Editorial Director   Arthur Hettich
Editor   Marie T. Walsh
Art Director   Joseph Taveroni
Decorating Editor   Carolyn Fleig
Associate Editor   Susan Kiely Tierney
Art Associate   Walter Schwartz
Assistant Editor   Ceri E. Hadda
Editorial Assistant   Raeanne B. Hytone
Production Manager   Kathy Maurer Reilly

BE YOUR OWN HOME DECORATOR

Decorating your home needn't be a time-consuming and expensive project. Today's trends in decorating give you the freedom to mix styles and reflect your own individual tastes. Your goal is to make your home work for *you*, without complicating your life style. Furnishings and fabrics must be as easy to maintain as they are beautiful to look at. Living spaces must be functional as well as comfortable. Here at last are practical, easy solutions to all your decorating problems. For example, see how plain kitchens are transformed with easy-care, inexpensive materials (page 2). You'll learn simple and imaginative ways to coordinate a room without making costly changes (page 67). See how colorful wallcovering can create an exciting mood in an often-ignored area of your home — the entrance hall (page 38). In the pages that follow, you'll find many great ideas for incorporating both comfort and practicality into your own decorating scheme.

THE GRAPHIC APPROACH
to bathroom design is easily achieved with coordinated sheets and towels. Here, a
Burlington sheet becomes a vivid shower curtain.
For project how-to's, see index on page 89.

Kitchens and bathrooms present unique problems for the home decorator. Most come with built-in fixtures, limiting design possibilities. With the ever-increasing interest in cooking, storage space for kitchen gadgets and utensils becomes crucial. And there just never seem to be enough shelves for towels and cosmetics in the bathroom. Add the more general limitations of budget, time or tools, and redecorating these rooms may seem an insurmountable task. With a bit of imagination, simple materials and surprisingly little money, you can make your kitchen and bathroom functional and attractive. Stretch space by adding storage units under and above sinks. Recycle furniture from basement or a junk shop to mix with modern equipment. Or camouflage worn pieces with several coats of paint.

KITCHENS & BATHS

RUSTIC barn siding and beams give warmth to a kitchen when recycled and used on cupboards and ceiling. Ceramic tiles complement wood tones.

SPANISH COUNTRY-STYLE KITCHEN

Armstrong designer Debbie Folsom created this idea-filled kitchen with nature in mind. Yet much of the room's natural appeal comes from man-made products. Old cabinets covered with Contact® paper have a warm wood tone. And the Armstrong flooring resembles hand-crafted tile. The simple-lined dining/work table and small chopping block are both rustic additions to the room, and ones you can make yourself. Imaginative use of rope unifies the country theme. Make a ladder wine rack or towel holder to utilize vertical space. Hang rope below a cupboard for extra storage. Or use it to make a "stained glass' window. Other ideas: Towel or utensil rack made from a dowel; burlap-hidden pots.

For project how-to's, see index on page 89.

5

WICKER
shelves and wood-
framed mirror replace
the more austere metal
medicine chest in
this cozy sink nook.
Note extra drawers below.

UTILITARIAN
space arrangements can
be visually pleasing, too.
Even narrow kitchens
can accommodate this
L-shaped work area, com-
plete with storage.
Display pots on the wall
for more room.

REJUVENATE
a tired-looking bathroom
with some simple changes.
Choose a lively wallcov-
ering, add a few pictures
and a mirror. Even play-up
an old-fashioned sink.

For project how-to's, see index on page 89.

6

COUNTRIFIED MULTI-PURPOSE ROOM

One room can function as several when space is at a premium. This 1877 house combines an open kitchen with dining and sitting areas. The informal arrangement ensures a steady flow of light, air and lots of good talk. Open shelving around windows and doors provides extra storage space.

COSMETIC CHANGES

Color coordination gives a standard bathroom new elegance. Plush towels and carpet by Fieldcrest complement a patterned wallcovering.

WALL TO WALL MIRROR

visually enlarges a small powder room, as does the built-in sink and vanity unit. Keep the lighting fixtures and wallcovering pattern delicate.

UNCLUTTERED kitchens require organized storage spaces. This streamlined kitchen stores all the equipment and food behind chrome-trimmed blue cabinets and centers around a cooking island.

OLD WORLD atmosphere in the kitchen below blends with modern convenience. Stainless steel counters, tile backsplashes and vinyl flooring are the new mates for the charming homespun accessories. Cabinets have been "antiqued" with paint for a finishing touch.

SLEEK SURFACES and ample storage space make this attractive bathroom more practical. The soft colors are enhanced by the unusual black sink and toilet.

EASY CARE surfaces in natural tones are as appealing as they are serviceable in this adobe-style kitchen. Hotpoint's new almond-colored appliances and sheet vinyl flooring make housework a breeze; ceramic tiles on counters and backsplashes are laid with soil-resistant grout.

MAKE THE MOST OF EVERY SPACE

When your kitchen is narrow, you have to consider all possible storage space. This galley kitchen utilizes often-ignored areas to advantage. It's equipped with lots of hanging storage, including a sliding hook system on the ceiling. Additional side wall hooks hold more cooking gear. Even the upper window ledge functions as a supplies area, displaying a neat row of spice bottles. Weathered wood is a decorative background, but it doesn't overpower the room.

DISPLAY YOUR WARES

Kitchen equipment can be an integral part of the decor, when everything's in open storage. Besides being a visually exciting arrangement, it's a time-saving one, too. Glassed-in cupboards let you take quick stock of dishes. (They can be made from less expensive woods.) Appliances are within easy reach, if they're left on the counter. Display your pots and pans, too; they add charm and eliminate clutter when hung from an iron rack on the ceiling. As a work/eating area, the butcher block island is additional counter space. A small window greenhouse completes the open effect of this kitchen. It lends a natural tone to the room, and lets light in.

UPDATED COUNTRY LOOK

This kitchen's old-fashioned wood motif mixes well with contemporary appliances. Natural wood cabinets, trimmed with seed-filled knobs, provide ample storage space. There's more room above and below the counter level of the work island.

VERY RUSTIC

Be innovative with decorating materials. In this bathroom, the rough texture of barn siding complements smooth ceramic tile. Easy care isn't sacrificed for good looks; the tile-lined shower and upper sink area clean like a breeze.

GIVE AN OLD PIECE NEW LIFE

Focal point in this Victorian bathroom: a recycled washstand combined with modern sink and fixtures. The room's original wood siding remains, painted green to match the coordinated wallcovering and fabric-covered shade.

COMBINATION LAUNDRY/BATHROOM

conserves space and saves you trips to the basement. Masonite® panels and louver doors handsomely conceal the stacked washer and dryer. The panels were also used to cover crumbling walls and make extra storage space. Designer Allen Scruggs chose GAF® flooring for its practicality and smart appearance. He also picked a floor-to-ceiling shower curtain to hide an old tub.

13

New ways with flooring and walls

CAMOUFLAGE homely bathroom tiles with contrasting color. In this pint-size area, a dreary ceramic design was hidden under Congoleum's shiny vinyl flooring. The beige wall tiles are livened with brown, picked up in the flooring and coordinated with Wall-Tex's wall-covering glued to the walls and ceiling. The storage unit built above the shower puts dead space to practical use. Projects start on page 17

CONNECT TWO AREAS with handsome flooring. Congoleum's vinyl flooring, adapted from a patchwork quilt, inspired Allen Scruggs' Early American decorating scheme that unites a galley kitchen and bare dining space. The window was heightened by Waverly's fabric repeated on the seats of Pennsylvania House's dining set. Projects, this page.

ABOVE-THE-SHOWER STORAGE UNIT

(page 14)

Here's a good-looking and practical way to make use of the wasted space above your shower. The ¾″ plywood shelf can be used to hide away the less frequently used items that so often clutter the bathroom. Doors can be rabbeted in ¾″ plywood, or assembled from ½″ and ¼″ plywood if power tools are not available. Materials and directions apply to the typical modern bath, which occupies an area of approximately 2½′x5′ with an 8′ ceiling. You may have to adjust these measurements, however, so that they suit your particular situation.

MATERIALS: Two ¾″ 4x8 sheets of exterior plywood (one ¾″, one ½″ and one ¼″ if using alternate method of making doors); 20 linear feet of 1x3 lumber; 10d common nails; 8d finishing nails; 8 offset hinges; 4 drawer pulls; 4 magnetic catches, plastic anchors ("Togglers") or other fastening devices as needed.

DIRECTIONS: Saw 1x3s to size to serve as cleats for the shelf (see Fig.

ABOVE-THE-SHOWER STORAGE UNIT
FIG. 1 FRAMING FOR TYPICAL BATH

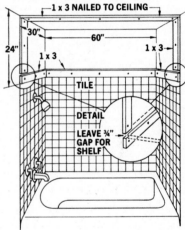

1). In many baths, the ceramic tile ends just above the shower head. When this is the case, install the 1x3s above the top of the tile. Nail the 10d nails at each corner and into the studs (upright framing members). If there are no studs at the ends of the side pieces, make a hole in the gypsum board and install plastic anchors. Nail into the anchors.

When the tile runs all the way to the ceiling, you will have to drill holes in the tile with a carbide drill bit, then install anchors into these holes. "Toggler" plastic anchors are good for either of these uses.

Saw the ¾″ plywood to fit on top of the cleats. (This job is much easier to do with a circular or saber saw.)

(Continued on page 17)

**Dress-up
plain-jane
bathrooms with
fabric and color**

(Continued from page 15)

Nail the plywood shelf to the cleats. Now take the distance across the front of the shelf, and measure from the ceiling to the bottom of the shelf. Cut the cabinet front from the plywood, with rectangular holes cut out, as shown in Fig. 2. You will probably

FIG. 2 CUTTING CABINET FRONT
¾" EXTERIOR PLYWOOD

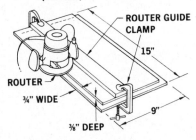

RUN CABINET FRONT DOWN TO
SHOWER DOORS OR CURTAIN ROD

want to run the bottom of the cabinet front down to the shower curtain rod or the top of the sliding door assembly as shown, for cosmetic purposes. If you do, be sure to locate the bottom of the openings in line with the top of the shelf. You might also want to consider venting the bottom of the cabinet with louvers, so steam from the shower can escape.

Professional-looking doors are made by rabbeting a groove around the edges as shown in Fig. 3A. Each

FIG. 3A RABBETTING CABINET DOORS (TYPICAL)

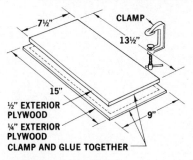

rabbet is ¾" in from the edge, and ⅜" deep. This can be done with a router or a table saw, but is very difficult to do without such equipment. Similar doors can be made by cutting the fronts of the doors out of ¼" plywood. Then cut out a backing from ½" plywood, ¾" less all around, and glue together with white glue and clamps (see Fig. 3B, page 22). Another alternate: Make flush doors from ½" plywood and use flush hinges. No matter which type is used, the outside dimensions of the doors should be ¾" wider on all sides than the openings

in the cabinet front.

Drill holes for drawer pulls and attach. Attach the doors to the cabinet front with hinges, then install the magnetic catches. Nail the whole assembly to the 1x3s as shown in Fig. 2, and also to the front of the shelf. Paint the assembled storage unit to match the decor in your bathroom; cover with wallcoverings, if you wish.

FIG. 3B MAKING CABINET DOORS WITH GLUE AND CLAMPS (TYPICAL DIMENSIONS)

CLAMP AND GLUE TOGETHER

SHOWER CURTAIN
(page 14)

If you want the patterns on the shower curtain to be at the same height as the ones on the walls, mark the curtain in the same manner as walls before you take it down. Otherwise, remove the curtain and make marks at two-inch intervals as desired. Lay the shower curtain flat on the floor, spreading newspapers around the edges where you will be spraying. If the curtain won't lay flat, tape or weight the corners. Make lines at 14-inch intervals, cross marking them every two inches as for walls. Using the same templates, spray paint from one side to the other. Allow at least 10 minutes for each color to dry before applying the next. Two coats may be required, depending on the material.

FABRIC-COVERED WINDOW CORNICE

(page 14)

Directions are given for a cornice that is 4' wide, but they can be easily adapted to your own situation. Since all the wood is covered, the cheapest grade interior plywood available or leftover scraps can be used.

MATERIALS: 1 sheet ¾" plywood; 4x4 or scrap if available; approximately 1 yard dacron batting sheet; approximately 1 yard cover fabric; ¼" or ½" cording; 2 or 3 L-brackets, depending on width; 4d finishing nails, white glue; staple gun.

DIRECTIONS: Making the Cornice — Cut out two pieces of plywood 6" wide and as long as the window width, plus any side moldings. Cut two pieces of plywood 5¼"x6" for the ends. Nail

PATTERNED SHEETS provide the materials for Gene Morin's easy-to-do bathroom projects. With a few pretty sheets you can cover the walls as well as radiator lid and boxes, and trim floor tiles and bath mat. Sew a curtain for the shower and shirr a sheet between two rods for the door. Extra storage can be created with an attractive antique bureau and baskets.

PEPPY COLOR such as a yellow accented with white can change a cold, high-ceiling bathroom into a cheerful setting. To break up the space, attach lattice screens below the ceiling and in front of the radiator, then curtain off the toilet.

6″   6″   5¼″

WIDTH OF WINDOW   6″

and glue the pieces together as shown in diagram on Nailing Plywood for Window Cornice. Cover the plywood by stapling dacron batting sheets to fit. **Applying Fabric** — Cut fabric to cover the cornice and staple on. Cut out 4″ strips of fabric on the bias, and make welting by using ¼″ to ½″ cording. Leave one edge of the welting about 1½ inches longer than the other. Staple the shorter edge of the welting onto the bottom edge of the cornice, then pull up the longer edge inside cornice and staple. Attach to molding or framing by screwing through the L-shaped brackets.

SEAT CUSHION

(page 14)

MATERIALS: Scrap fabric or sheet, size depending on the dimensions of your chairs and the number of cushions you wish to make (see SHEET YARDAGE CHART, page 000); large piece of tracing paper; ¼″ cording; polyester fiberfill for stuffing.
DIRECTIONS: Trace an outline of chair seat onto tracing paper, leaving 1″ extra all around for hem. Cut two pieces of fabric to this size for the back and front panels of cushion case. **To Make Piping** — Cut on the bias from another piece of fabric a strip 3″ wide and as long as your size pillow will require. Enclose ¼″ cording in bias strip and machine stitch directly next to cording, leaving a hem to be sewn into cushion case. **To Make Ties** — Cut four 2″-wide strips of fabric 12″ long along selvage edge and fold right sides together; stitch with a ¼″ seam; turn right-side out; press; turn one raw edge under. **Sewing Cushion Case** — Take one fabric panel for cushion case and place cording on one edge of the right side of the fabric, with hem of cording facing outward. Machine stitch cording to panel on all 4 sides. Then place the right sides of the 2 back and front panels together. On each back corner of cushion, place 2 tie strips, raw edges at corner, so that there will be 2 streamers on each corner to attach pillow to chair. Starting with one of these corners, machine stitch all around, ending with the other corner, and leaving an opening for the fiberfill. Then turn pillow right-side out and stuff with fiberfill, making sure corners are well packed. Sew opening closed with machine or by hand.

MAKING DRAPERIES WITH FABRIC

You can add a decorator's touch to rooms by choosing fabric to go with your rug, sofa, chairs and wallcovering, then making draperies that fit each window perfectly.
MATERIALS: Drapery fabric (we used "Poppies" by Riverdale); fabric for lining; yardstick or metal tape measure; matching thread; pleater tape; dressmaker pins; pleater hooks; sharp scissors.
DIRECTIONS — Determining the Amount of Fabric Needed:
1. Draperies are measured to fit window hardware, rather than the window itself, so install hardware if it is not already in place.
2. Decide the length you wish the draperies to be. (The usual lengths are to the window sill, window apron or floor length, subtracting ½″ to clear the floor and more, if there is baseboard heat.)
3. With yardstick or metal tape measure, measure the length from the top of the drapery rod to the chosen length for the draperies; to this add 7″ for hems and length taken up by fullness.
4. Measure the width of drapery rod; add the distance from bend in rod to wall, the space for the overlap (if it is a traverse rod) and 3″ for side hem. This number doubled is the fabric width required for each window. If the window is 36″ wide, the distance from bend in rod to wall is 4″ and the overlap is 4″, the total width of fabric for the window would be twice the total of 36″ + 4″ (bend in rod) +4″ (overlap) +3″ (side hem), or 94″. Divide this number in half for the width of each drapery. (Since half of 94″ is 47″ and our fabric is 48″ wide, 1 width of fabric was needed for each drapery.) For wider windows, divide the drapery width by the width of the fabric and adjust to the nearest whole number for the number of panels required to make each drapery.
5. To estimate the total amount of fabric required, multiply the number of panels by the total length for each panel and divide by 36″. (If you choose floor-length draperies with 86″ + 7″ for hems, you will need twice 93″ or 186″ divided by 36″, or a total of 5¼ yds.)
6. For lining, use above fabric measurements, except reduce the width by 6″ and the length by 2½″.
(Note: These measurements do not take into account patterns that need to be matched. If this is necessary, measure the number of inches between pattern repeats and add this

number to the length of *each* panel.)
Sewing:
1. Cut drapery and lining fabric to measured length for each panel. Sew panels together, if necessary, to obtain desired width for each drape, using a ½″ seam; press seams open.
2. Stitch a 1″ hem along lining bottom; pin drapery and lining fabrics, right sides together, along left side; stitch from top to within 2″ of lining bottom with a ½″ seam.
3. Pull lining fabric over so that its edge meets edge of drapery fabric; pin; stitch with ½″ seam to within 2″ of bottom of lining.
4. Center lining on drapery and press seams towards lining. Turn drapery hem up 3″ over lining; stitch ½″ seam down to bottom on each edge; turn drapery right-side out; slip stitch drapery hem. Tack facing to hem and hem to lining.
5. Turn top edge of drapery down 3″; press; pin pleater tape ¼″ down from top edge. Stitch along top and bottom of tape, keeping the cut ends turned under. *Do not* stitch pockets closed.
6. Insert pleater hooks and hang draperies in curtain hardware, arranging folds carefully.

FABRIC-DRAPED TABLE

A battered round table can be turned into decorative furniture with a smashing cloth covering. Follow these easy directions, using fabric or a sheet.
MATERIALS: Fabric (we used "Basketry" by Riverdale); tape measure; sharp scissors; string; pencil; matching thread.
DIRECTIONS: Determining Amount of Fabric Needed — Measure the diameter of the table, then the distance from table top to floor. For length and width of fabric needed, add diameter of table, plus 2 times the distance from table top to floor, plus 1″ for hem. (If your table is 30″ in diameter and 28″ from table top to floor, it would be 30″ + 2x28″ + 1″, or 87″.) For fabric not wide enough: Divide width needed by the width of fabric and multiply by the length for total fabric needed. Since our fabric is 48″ wide, we needed 2 widths of fabric times 87″; divided by 36″, this makes 5 yds. (If you're working with sheets, see SHEET YARDAGE CHART on page 90 for sheet size required to cover table.)
Making Cloth — When fabric is not of the width required, cut into required lengths. Cut one piece in half, lengthwise. Stitch one length to each side of uncut fabric with a ½″ seam. Press seams open. (This gives the

(Continued on page 37)

ABC'S OF FURNITURE CARE

Your furniture can give you years of enjoyment if it's cared for properly. Regular cleaning, waxing and polishing are generally all that's required, plus having a few simple remedies on hand for any damages that should occur. But first, a few words about preventive care:

- Keep furniture away from strong sunlight.
- Wipe up spilled foods and beverages immediately—don't allow them to dry and get absorbed into the finish.
- Don't place hot dishes or an object with rubber feet directly on the furniture surface.
- Use coasters under glasses, flowerpots and vases.
- Don't keep vinyl plastic pads or place mats on furniture for any length of time.

MAINTENANCE OF WOOD FURNITURE

Waxing and polishing is essential for maintaining the beauty of wood. You can use the same product on both light and dark woods, for it's really the finish on the piece that you're protecting, not the wood. The films of lacquer used to seal modern furniture provide their own protective surface and usually prevent cleaning agents from penetrating the wood. It's the type and condition of this finish, the amount of shine you want, as well as your own preference for one method over another that should determine the product you choose. There are three kinds of waxes: *Aerosol* wax, one of the most popular today, is the easiest to use and gives both cleansing and protective action; *liquid* wax gives a sanitizing effect to surfaces; *paste* waxes create a very durable finish, can help camouflage minor damage and are good cleaners. Some of these products produce high gloss while others give a more satiny look, so check the labels on the cans to make sure you buy the right one for your piece of furniture—and follow the manufacturer's directions carefully.

Wood furniture also requires periodic cleaning. If a piece begins to look streaky and cloudy, it may mean that wax has been improperly or too generously applied. An accumulation of grease from cooking might be another cause. Whatever the problem, never clean wood with soap and water. The best furniture cleaners are either a good wax or a household solvent such as odorless mineral spirits or naphtha (which can be bought in paint stores or in the hardware section of department stores).

To clean with wax: Choose an aerosol or liquid wax and use a soft cloth made out of cotton (a discarded handkerchief, sheet, diaper or undershirt are all good for this purpose). The cloth should be absorbent and free of lint. Fold the cloth into a pad about the size of your palm; saturate the cloth with wax (if you're using an aerosol, apply directly to a small area of the furniture surface), using enough wax to wet the area thoroughly. With a circular motion, clean a small area at a time, making the final stroke follow the direction of the grain in the wood. Wipe area dry immediately with a clean cloth while the wax is still moist. Switch to fresh cloths any time the one you're using becomes too damp. Your final wipe, again, should go in the direction of the grain. After cleaning, polish with wax according to label directions.

To clean with mineral spirits or naphtha: Saturate a soft, clean, folded cloth with a generous amount of solvent; rub over a small area with a circular motion, cleaning well. Remove soil and old wax with a clean, dry cloth, changing cloths often, until the cloth comes away clean. Now wax the surface.

If your furniture has carved designs or is intricately decorated, applying wax and polish using the normal methods may be difficult. Instead, dust these areas with a cloth that's been slightly moistened with a liquid or spray wax, or clean with a wax-moistened cotton swab.

(Note: Some people prefer to use lemon oil for cleaning and polishing their wood furniture, and this is fine. However it's important that, whichever method you choose, you stick with it. If you switch from one to another, your furniture will become streaked and dulled.)

Remedies for Minor Trouble Spots:

Even with the best of care, accidents do happen and you may find yourself with a piece of furniture that's been scratched or otherwise marred. In the event of extensive trouble, the piece may have to be refinished, but there are some do-it-yourself cures for minor damages. If the mar has not penetrated the finish, simply applying furniture wax will often hide it. Or try first rubbing the area gently with a little paste wax applied with a fine grade 3/0 steel wool, then polishing. If these methods fail, the following treatments may prove helpful. (Before applying any of them, remove all wax from the finish by rubbing the area with a cloth soaked in naphtha or odorless mineral spirits, then dry with a clean cloth.)

- Nut meats or linseed oil provide enough color to cover a minor scratch. Break a raw Brazil nut or black walnut in half and rub the meat well into the mar. If you use linseed oil, apply it with a clean cloth.
- Coloring crayons or wax sticks in the appropriate color can be useful in hiding blemishes.
- Liquid shoe polish comes in a variety of shades and you can get some that is very close in color to walnut and oak. Apply the polish with a cotton swab, then buff.
- A mixture of iodine and mercurochrome will resemble the color of mahogany or maple.
- Rottenstone and oil can provide another effective camouflage. You can obtain rottenstone from a paint or hardware store; get about an ounce and keep it stored in an old salt shaker or spice container for emergencies. To use, sprinkle a few drops of lubricating or salad oil on the scratch, then shake on enough rottenstone to make a pasty substance. Rub briskly with a soft, clean cloth, following the direction of the grain in the wood. Wipe often to compare and match the gloss of the camouflaged area with the original finish.

For More Serious Damage:

If the damage is deeper, the treatment will be a little more complicated, but it's worth a try if you want to avoid completely refinishing the item. Here are some of the more common mishaps that may occur and what to do about them:

Cigarette Burns—Clean the burned area by scraping it with a sharp knife or single-edge razor blade, removing any charred wood. Then clean well with a cotton swab dipped in odorless mineral spirits or naphtha. Next, smooth the surface with 3/0 steel wool wrapped around the pointed edge of an orange stick and clean again. Rub once more, going with the grain, but this time use a very fine sandpaper or emery board. Apply some stain. When the stain is dry, you can fill in the damaged area with stick shellac that matches the color of the wood finish. Here's how: Heat a spatula over an electric heating unit until it's just warm enough to melt the shellac. Scrape a bit of the shellac off the stick with the blade and press into the damaged area, repeating until it's filled. To smooth the surface, clean the spatula and run it across the area

(Continued on page 37)

HOW TO GET THE MOST FROM YOUR DECORATING DOLLARS

The word "home" brings to mind so many pleasant associations — kids laughing, merry discussions around the dinner table, quiet times curled up on the couch watching T.V., the freedom to be yourself. In short, it's a special place that belongs to you and your family alone. Naturally, you take pride in the way it looks, the atmosphere of warmth it generates, and want it to reflect your own special tastes. But while there are so many decorating ideas to choose from, only you can decide what appeals to you and what works for you. So before you begin any decorating project, it's a good idea to ask yourself a few questions about your own particular needs and how much money and time you want to spend in making your home everything you want it to be. Finding out what's available and getting the best value for your money are the next important steps.

Among the first things to consider are your style of living and what you feel most comfortable with. Do you like a formal or a more casual atmosphere? Are you more at home with large, stately furniture and showy rooms or more free-flowing, livable surroundings? The actual time you spend in your home is another factor. If both you and your husband work, there isn't much time to be fussing with housework, so you'll need to concentrate on convenience — well-organized kitchens where utensils can be reached in a hurry, easy-to-care-for furnishings and carpets. And how about your kids? Are they toddlers and likely to turn your living room into a playground at a moment's notice? Then you probably won't want to risk putting a white rug on the floor or have your couch covered with a delicate, hard-to-care-for fabric.

How frequently you entertain overnight guests, the need for private study or reading areas for you and the children, and the amount of freedom your lively dog or cat has in the house are also important considerations in your choice of furnishings, your use of space and even the colors you decide upon. But the great thing about do-it-yourself decorating is that the results will reflect your own tastes and individuality. With a little experimenting, you're sure to come up with a decor that's aesthetically pleasing as well as practical. And since it's no longer necessary to decorate in only one style, you can have the fun of mixing and matching the best of many periods and styles.

Making a Floor Plan

Next comes the actual working out of it all. You'll need to assess the layout of your house or apartment, the space you're working with in each room, and note the locations of certain fixtures like electric sockets, windows, doors, fireplaces and radiators. If you're only doing a bit of remodeling, you'll want to coordinate any new furnishings with what you already have. In order to make an accurate evaluation of how everything will fit, a floor plan is essential. Outline each room on graph paper, making each square equal one foot, and note the exact position of built-in features. Also record wall length and ceiling height (a folding ruler or metal tape measure provides the most accurate measurements). Once you've got your room on paper, you can toy with ideas of where furniture can be best placed for attractiveness and maneuverability. While you're in the planning stage, keep these points in mind:

• Allow enough space to maneuver around. There should be enough leeway to walk comfortably through a room, around tables and chairs, to windows and so on. Plan traffic lanes of about two feet in width, about three feet at doorways.

• Furnishings should relate to each other in size and to the size of the room. Large pieces will overpower a small room; delicate-looking furniture will get lost in a large room.

• Decide what you want to make the focal center of the room, e.g., a window, fireplace or some other built-in feature, and arrange pieces of furniture accordingly.

• When deciding on textures of fabrics for upholstery, floor and wallcoverings, realize that having them both match and contrast creates a more subtle look than having everything match perfectly or contrast sharply.

• Make color work for you. The creative use of color can add magic to a room and influence your mood, too. It's a good idea to create a color scheme from your favorite colors rather than putting them together randomly. You may want to set up rooms in a related scheme (colors that fall next to each other on the color wheel, e.g., blue and green), monochromatic scheme (tints and shades of a single color) or complementary scheme (opposites on the color wheel, e.g. blue and orange).

• Keep seating pieces in cohesive groups.

• Provide some pull-up chairs.

• Very large rooms can be broken up with area rugs.

• Don't feel you have to fill up every available space with furniture. Allow some breathing room.

Invest Wisely in Furniture

Once you've decided what changes to make, you'll want to shop around for what you need. Since furniture can be expensive, it's important to make the wisest choices for your money. You don't need the most costly pieces to make your home functional and attractive, but there are some general features to look for when shopping to assure yourself of quality. (Note: Any piece you buy should have labels explaining the kinds of wood and/or fabric used, an indication of any simulations of hand-carved trims or other decorative features and maintenance information—so read them carefully.)

Good construction of any piece of furniture depends on how well the parts have been put together. Secure joints are crucial on pieces that will receive heavy wear—a chair or dining table, for example. Any moving hinges, table slides, etc. should be made of heavy metal that works smoothly and quietly. The best-quality drawers are hand-fitted and can be closed easily by pushing lightly on one corner; the interior should be smoothly sanded and sealed. Also look for dust panels between drawers —thin sheets of plywood that keep out dust and separate the contents of one drawer from those of another. Check the entire piece—underneath, in the back and on the sides—for defects or rough finishes, and tap each panel with your fingers to be sure it doesn't rattle or feel loose. Framing on the backs of cabinets, chests and drawers is another sign of quality. This feature makes the piece stronger as well as dust-proof. The finish on a piece of wooden furniture should also receive careful inspection. Look for a clear sheen, rather than a hard gloss, and make sure that the front, top and sides of the item blend in color and graining.

Besides looking at and touching each piece carefully, test it out. Sit in
(Continued on page 37)

GLOSSARY
OF DECORATING TERMS

Acrylic—A synthetic fiber with a soft, wooly texture; creates a plush look.

Apron—Supportive and decorative boxing that connects the legs on a piece of furniture to the body; in a window, the molding under the sill.

American Traditional—Decorating style dating from the homespun furnishings of the first American settlers through the styles of the 19th century.

Backing—Strong material into which carpet yarns are tufted; sometimes latex-coated.

Basket weave—A simple, flat fabric that gives the appearance of a woven basket.

Batik—A fabric, usually cotton, that's handpainted and made by dipping the fabric into dyes after the designs have been coated with wax.

Brocade—Rich silk-textured and shiny fabric with a raised design, usually floral, and often embroidered in many colors.

Bentwood—Furniture made of wood that has been softened, then curved into the desired shape.

Broadloom—A term of measurement for carpet wider than six feet.

Cane—A flexible material made from rattan that has been split into narrow strands and woven into the backs and seats of chairs.

Cabriole—A furniture leg shaped in curves with the top and ball curved out and the center curved in. Common in Queen Anne and Chippendale styles.

Campaign chest—Easily portable furniture with metal corners and handles similar to those used on 18th century miliary chests.

Chintz—A flat fabric which has been treated to give it a polished look, usually printed with a floral design.

Commode—A low chest of drawers.

Contemporary—Furnishings designed and made today.

Cornice—A decorative frame used to conceal drapery hardware.

Crewel work—Bright, bold embroidery using worsted yarn, generally in a mixture of English and East Indian motifs based on the tree of life design.

Damask—Patterns imitating stylized textile motifs in which foliage predominates; often seen in two-tone color ways.

Découpage—The decorating of an object with paper or fabric cutouts that are glued on and finished with several layers of shellac.

Dowel—A headless pin, usually made of wood, used in the construction of furniture.

Director's chair—A chair that has a wooden frame and usually, a fabric seat and cross-legged base.

Distress—Furniture that has been marred artifically and finished to look aged.

Early American—Decorating style that incorporates rustic furniture of first American settlers (1608-1720); also can mean the American version of 17th century English styles.

Eclectic—A mixture of furnishings from different periods and places.

Faux bamboo—Simulated bamboo used in furniture making.

Flat weave—Fabric that has no pile but may be course and nubby due to the differnt sizes of yarns used.

Georgian—Taken from 18th century English design, this is one of the most popular styles produced in America. As made in this country, the style includes the Chippendale, Sheraton and Heppelwhite designs.

Gimp—A narrow, decorative trimming used for general ornamentation and to cover upholstery nails.

Grass cloth—Originally, a handmade product, often imported from Japan, and made by gluing woven grasses onto a paper backing.

Highboy—A tall chest of drawers mounted on a long-legged commode.

Inlay—Wood, metal, ivory or other material set into a surface to achieve a decorative effect.

Louis XV—The King of France from 1715 to 1774; his name is used to describe the furniture having delicate curvilinear lines that was popular during his reign.

Louis XVI—French king (1774-1793); describes furniture with straight lines and classic motifs.

Lacquer—A glossy, often resinous, material that is applied to surfaces in thin layers and polished to a high shine.

Modern—A streamlined approach to furnishings that eliminates unnecessary frills and emphasizes current materials used, such as steel, glass and plastics.

Modular—Furniture components that can be used separately or combined as needed.

Molding—A contoured strip of wood, metal, plastic or plaster that is applied to doors, windows, walls or furniture for an ornamental effect.

Mural—A large picture painted on a wall or applied to a wallcovering.

Parquet—An inlaid woodwork design used on floors and furniture surfaces.

Parsons table—A classic square or rectangular table with apron and legs the same width.

Patina—The sheen on furniture surfaces produced by age and use; the change is usually to a more mellow color than the original. It can be achieved by artificial means.

Olefin—A fiber made from petroleum by-products; it's lightweight and long-wearing and is usually used in carpets, slipcovers and upholstery fabrics.

Provincial—Rustic versions of the more sophisticated furniture popular in cities, made in the provinces or country.

Queen Anne—Style during reign of Queen Anne of England (1720-1750) featuring small, delicately proportioned furniture with accented curves, cabriole legs, carved shell designs, scrolled bracket feet, and sunburst and fan motifs.

Rattan—An Oriental palm woven into wicker-work furniture.

Relief—Ornament above the surface it decorates.

Repeat—The size of one complete pattern on a fabric, wallcovering or carpet.

Sectional—Seating designed to be used separately or grouped together.

Selvage—Woven edge of a piece of fabric.

Sisal—Straw-like fiber from a tropical plant used for padding or for lightweight rugs.

Side chair—An armless dining chair.

Tester—A canopy on a four-poster bed.

Traditional—Style of decorating inspired by the past.

Tufting—A method of locking yarns on the surface. These loops can then be cut to create a velvet suuface.

Valance—An ornamental horizontal strip across a window top that conceals drapery hardware.

Value—The lightness or darkness of a color.

Veneer—A thin layer of attractively grained wood or other material applied over a less attractive wood.

Welting—Covered cording that joins sections of upholstery, or creates a neat finish where the upholstery joins wood surfaces.

Windsor chair—A chair with bentwood back frame, turnings on the back for support and pegged legs set into a saddle-shaped seat.

Wing chair—An overstuffed chair with projecting sides on the high upholstered back.

MAKE A FRAME in highly styled Art Deco design for an incredibly low price. The shiny frame is clear glass sprayed with coats of Krylon paint and decorated with several strips of aluminum tape.

RECYCLE a beat-up desk with two cans of Krylon spray paint and aluminum tape. This desk was patched, sprayed and taped with a chevron design and looks like a million.

Make a collection of
fabulous furnishings with
limited time and money

SUPER LAMPS are a cinch to make. These cost only a few dollars to put together and can brighten up any room with their lively Americana designs featuring a whale of a cutout and a Pennsylvania Dutch motif, for just starters. The materials that make the lamps shine are all standard parts. How-tos start on page 35.

Create a grand illusion with simple, do-it-yourself projects. In less time than imagined, you can make custom-designed furnishings that look expensive, but cost little to produce. With only beginner's skills and household equipment it's easy to turn raw wood furniture into one-of-a-kind designs, add your own personal touch to store-bought accessories, or create useful items from a few pieces of plywood.

NEW PROJECTS TO MAKE

EASY LIVING is achieved in an enclosed back porch that's in bloom all year round. A natural, inviting mood is created with lots of greenery teamed with casual wicker furniture. It's an easy-care look, too— even the bright sofa fabric is stain resistant.

PORCHES

If the need for an extra room is your problem, check out your porch! Glassed in or left wide open, your porch represents a possible family room, living room or even dining room that offers casual, wide-open space for informal entertaining.

**OPEN
PORCH**
with informal white
wicker chairs and a
refurbished park
bench offers a
panoramic view you
wouldn't have indoors.
And notice the small
amount of space this
extra room occupies.

**THE TURN-OF-
THE-CENTURY**
charm of designer
Everett Brown's
front porch makes
it one of his favorite
rooms. And no wonder—
it's so warm and
inviting, arranged with
wicker furniture and
Royal Doulton china.

27

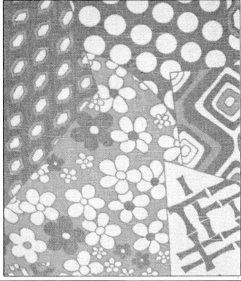

THE COLORS OF NATURE
as viewed from this spacious porch, are reflected in the bright greens, pinks and oranges used indoors. Sliding glass doors make this an all-year-round family room, while the easy-care upholstery fabrics make it practical as well.

FRESH GREEN

in a practical vinyl fabric on chairs and sofa, is a cool backdrop for outdoor dining. Coffee table is put to good use as an extra buffet area.

PERSIAN GARDEN

is the overriding theme of this vibrant fabric. Cool garden imagery is combined with easy Scotchgard® maintenance, making this a practical choice for family living.

YEAR-ROUND

porch by designer Diane Saxton is viewed through the living room window. An informal look is achieved with a serviceable tile floor and cool blues mixed with nature's greenery.

SUBTLE PLAID

gives interest to this vanilla velvet fabric. And when specially treated, velvet becomes practical enough to use throughout the house.

IRIS APPLIQUÉ QUILT

MATERIALS: Two white twin-size sheets (percale); percale or broadcloth (36" or 45" wide), ¼ yard each of lemon, old gold, lavender, royal purple, light blue, medium blue, medium pink, light red, 2 yards grass green; thread to match each color; one batt twin-size polyester quilt filling; paper for pattern; cardboard (file folder weight); scissors; ruler; straight pins; sharp, soft pencil; needle; dry ballpoint pen and dressmaker's carbon paper; iron.

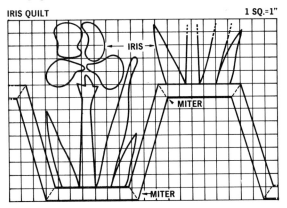

IRIS QUILT   1 SQ.=1"

DIRECTIONS: Remove all stitching from sheets (open hems). Shrink all fabrics and sheets. Dry. Iron. Put one sheet aside. Take second sheet and fold it lengthwise to find center. Mark center with basting stitch. Fold sheet crosswise to find center line. Mark with stitching line. Open sheet out, right side up, on large flat surface. Using placement sketch as guide, lightly mark the location of the green bands which separate the iris. Cut strips of green fabric lengthwise of the material and 1½" wide. Turn in ¼" on each long side and press. Baste turn in to hold in place but keep knots on the right side so that the basting can be removed easily later. Pin strips as indicated by marks and baste in place. Miter corners as shown. There will be "incomplete" sections at top and bottom of quilt which could hold half an iris but are instead left empty. Make paper patterns for iris petals and leaves. Each leaf is separate piece as is stem. Using dressmaker's carbon paper and dry ball point pen, transfer the patterns to *wrong* side of fabric in colors shown.

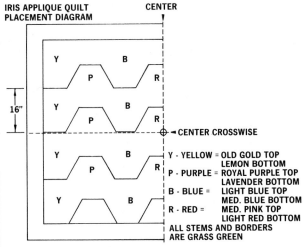

IRIS APPLIQUE QUILT PLACEMENT DIAGRAM   CENTER

16"

CENTER CROSSWISE

Y - YELLOW = OLD GOLD TOP
                LEMON BOTTOM
P - PURPLE = ROYAL PURPLE TOP
                LAVENDER BOTTOM
B - BLUE =   LIGHT BLUE TOP
                MED. BLUE BOTTOM
R - RED =   MED. PINK TOP
                LIGHT RED BOTTOM
ALL STEMS AND BORDERS ARE GRASS GREEN

Cut out pieces allowing additional ¼" for turn in. Make cardboard pattern for each part of iris and leaves and cut them out. Place cardboard piece on wrong side of matching cut out fabric piece with excess fabric extending equally on all edges. Bring this excess over the cardboard and press. Remove cardboard piece. Baste the pressed-down excess to keep it firmly in place. Repeat until all pieces are pressed and basted. Pin pieces, right side up, to sheet, using pattern as guide. Stitch

invisibly to sheet. When all are finished, position side, top and bottom strips of green as shown, removing any portions of crosswise bands which extend. These strips are 2" wide (1½" when finished). The side strips almost touch the iris leaf nearest the edge. Finish stitching all green bands. Remove all basting stitches. Cut green bands for outer border 3½" wide. Turn in one long edge (¼") and press and baste. Sew basted edge 4" from edge of inner border. If there is excess sheeting, trim off all but 1" from the stitching line. Place finished appliqué, right side down. Open quilt filling and arrange it centered on sheet. Place other sheet, right side up, on the filling. Pin all layers together thoroughly. If the appliquéd sheet had any fabric trimmed from it, trim the lining sheet in the same way. Turn green outer border to lining side so that there is only 1½" on the right side. Stitch in place. Turn quilt right side up and lightly catch stitch top and backing (through filling) along the green fabric lines. (**Note:** When turning under allowance for flower appliqué, just before final sewing, slash the turned-under portion where necessary to ease fabric.)

CREWEL CHAIR CUSHION AND FOOTSTOOL

MATERIALS: Pure Irish linen or homespun (fabric should be 5" larger than cushion or footstool on all sides to allow for assembling); crewel wool in the following colors: dark green, light green, dark blue, light blue, gray, purple, medium pink, light pink, red, yellow, orange and rust; crewel needle; pencil; tracing paper; dressmaker's carbon.

CREWEL FOOTSTOOL   1 SQ.=1"

DIRECTIONS: Following directions on page 37, enlarge pattern onto paper. Transfer design to Irish linen or homespun, using dressmaker's carbon. Refer to photograph on cover for color guide. Also refer to Stitch Guide on page 128 for Roumanian Couching and Trellis Couching. **For Footstool:** Flower stems are worked in the Stem or Outline Stitch in dark green and light green. Leaves and large stems are worked in Roumanian Couching in dark green and light green; border designs in dark blue, light blue and gray. Bugs are worked in Trellis Couching. Flowers are worked in Roumanian Couching, their centers in Trellis Couching and French Knots. Colors are orange, yellow, medium pink, light pink, red and dark blue. **For Chair Cushion:** Berries are worked in Roumanian Couching in purple, dark blue and worked in Trellis Couching in various combinations of dark blue, light blue, gray, orange and rust. Bottom border is worked in Roumanian Couching in dark blue, light blue and gray. Use the Outline Stitch to add additional color and emphasis of design to flowers, bugs and leaves.

NATURAL LOOK KITCHEN

(pages 4-5)

TOWEL BAR
MATERIALS: ¾" poplar; ⅞" dowel; stain; varnish.

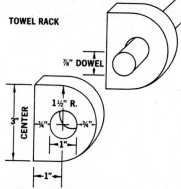

DIRECTIONS: See diagram for towel bar assembly. When completed, stain and varnish.

ROPE TOWEL RACK
MATERIALS: 1" manila rope; ¾" dowel, cut into 12" lengths.

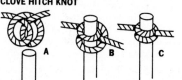

DIRECTIONS: Our towel rack is basically a rope ladder with ¾" dowels used for the rungs. The ladder is made from a single piece of rope folded in half. It can be hung from a cabinet or wall and made to whatever length you choose. The dowels are secured to the rope with a clove hitch knot (see diagram). The knot is formed (A); the dowel is inserted into knot (B); the ends are then pulled tight (C). The dowels are attached at right angles to the rope and parallel to each other at 12" to 14" intervals. Fasten each dowel at both ends before moving on to the next.

CREWEL CHAIR CUSHION   1 SQ.=1"

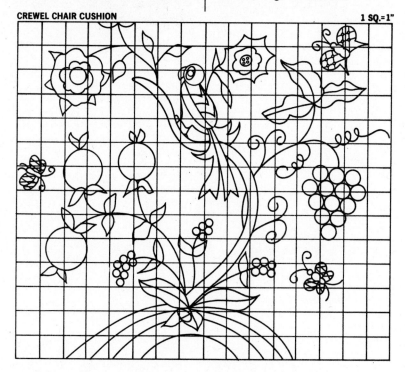

medium pink. Leaves are Roumanian Couching in dark and light green. Flower stems are worked in Stem or Outline Stitch in dark and light green. Large central stem is Roumanian Couching in dark blue. Parrot is worked in Roumanian Couching in dark green, light green, dark blue and light blue, with orange beak and claws. Flowers are worked in Roumanian Couching in medium pink, light pink and yellow. Flower centers are worked in Trellis Couching and French Knots in orange. Bugs are

SHOWER CURTAIN

(page 2)

MATERIALS: One twin flat sheet; plastic curtain liner; large eyelets or grommets; shower curtain hooks; 6' of stiff pellon or drapery header.
DIRECTIONS: Leave the top hem in place. Measure 6' down the side edge (selvage) of the sheet, plus 6" more for hem. Cut the sheet at this point. Press in a double 3" hem; slip pellon within the folds; stitch hem closed with sewing machine or by hand. Apply grommets or large eyelets, or make machine buttonholes to coincide with eyelets on plastic liner you'll hang behind curtain. Lay curtain and liner together; put curtain hooks through both. Hang on curtain rod.

GRAPHIC DESIGN WALL

(page 2)

MATERIALS: Tape measure; level; pencil; metal-edged ruler; latex semi-gloss enamel; paint rollers; poly brush (flat polyester sponge brush sold in paint stores).
DIRECTIONS: Before painting a graphic design on walls or ceiling, make a sample stripe from wrapping paper to make sure the size of the graphic is in correct proportion to the room. (This does not have to be a complete design but just a portion.) When you have decided the size and placement of your graphic, use tape measure, pencil and level to measure lines from either floor or ceiling, depending on how close your stripe will be to either. With pencil and tape measure, place small marks on wall, 2 feet apart. With level, check the accuracy. You may have to follow the ceiling line (especially with a stripe close to the ceiling,) whether it is level or not. Draw lines with a metal-edged ruler. Use any commercial latex semi-gloss enamel (very washable for kitchen and retards mildew in bathroom). Paint the main wall area (not the graphic) using a roller. With poly brush, cut in edges of graphic carefully. Use another roller to fill in middle of graphic.

PINE-LOOK CABINETS
The look of wood paneling was achieved easily and inexpensively with Contact® paper. We used Knotty Pine #130E. First the cabinets were given a coat of paint in a dark color to contrast with the pine. The Contact® paper was cut on the bias, following cutting lines already printed on the paper backing. It was then applied in strips on the diagonal, leaving a narrow strip of painted cabinet visible between each Contact® strip. To finish, carefully trim all edges.

ROPE WINE RACK
MATERIALS: Plywood panel large enough to face existing cabinet; 1" manila rope; cup hooks.

DIRECTIONS: Attach plywood panel from counter to ceiling, 6″ out from existing cabinet. The wine rack is formed by rope which is looped around cup hooks and "laced" from ceiling to counter. One complete lacing is made in front, as shown in diagram; and another is made approximately 8″ behind it. Cup hooks are screwed in 6″ apart (see diagram).

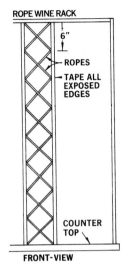

ROPE WINE RACK

6″
ROPES
TAPE ALL EXPOSED EDGES
COUNTER TOP

FRONT-VIEW

BUTCHER BLOCK TABLE
MATERIALS: 1″x4″ poplar; ¾″x3″ poplar laminated to 3″ square for legs; butcher block formica; copper corner plates; square head ornamental screws; ¼″ R.H. bolts; miter box; stain; varnish.

BUTCHER BLOCK TABLE
CONSTRUCT SAME AS TABLE TOP INCLUDING COPPER CORNERS

18″   18″
4″
¾″ x 1½″
36″   36″
4″
3″
¾″   30″
4″   POPLAR
BUTCHER BLOCK PLASTIC LAMINATE ON ¾″ FIR PLYWOOD
3″   3″
¼″ R.H. BOLTS
COPPER (4) CORNERS

DIRECTIONS: See diagram for butcher block table assembly. When completed, stain and varnish.

SPANISH COURT TILE INSTALLATION

(page 4-5)

MATERIALS: Hammer; nails; string; chalk; carpenter's square; Armstrong Stylistic® adhesive-backed vinyl floor tiles (12″x12″ each; multiply width of floor surface times length and add 10% to this figure); paper; pencil, heavy shears or utility knife. (**Note:** We used Spanish Court Pattern #28011 Caramel. Keeping the tiles and room at 70°F for 48 hours before laying the tiles will assure easy handling.)

DIRECTIONS—Preparing Floor: First remove quarter-round molding or cove base, if any; set aside for later reinstallation. Floor surface must be dry and smooth without dust, grease or wax build-up. Here's how to prepare different types of floors:

• If floor is concrete, it must be smooth, dry and clean; fill in all holes and cracks. Don't install tiles over existing flooring on concrete slabs in contact with earth.

• If floor is concrete and painted with an oil base paint, remove all traces of paint; rubber base (latex) paint needn't be removed if it is free of blisters and peeling.

• Any old smooth-surface, non-foam floor covering can be left as the subfloor, but it must be tightly adhered. Remove all surface coatings with strong detergent solution and rinse and dry thoroughly. When installing tiles over old resilient tile flooring material, make sure the joints of the new flooring don't align with those of the old floor beneath.

• If floors are wood, they must be firm and smooth, with at least 18″-deep cross-ventilated air spaces beneath them. Replace badly worn boards; renail any loose boards. Double-layer strip wood floors with top boards 3″ or less in width must be covered with ¼″ underlayment hardboard or ¼″ underlayment grade plywood. Single wood floors must be covered with ⅜″ or heavier underlayment grade plywood. Use annular nails with all nail heads driven flush or slightly below the underlayment board surface. Do *not* use lining felt over underlayment hardboard or plywood.

Measuring the Room:
1. Since the corners of a room are seldom right angles, it is best to install the tiles starting from the center of the room. To find the center, measure the length of each side of the room and drive a nail into the floor (if wood) or mark the floor (if concrete) at the center of each of these side walls. Disregard bays, alcoves or other irregularities in the walls.

2. Connect the center points of two opposite side walls by tightly stretching a chalked string between these points and snapping it against the floor. Measure along this chalkline and mark its center point. With a carpenter's square or a loose tile as a guide, snap a second chalkline at right angles to the first, crossing at the center point. It is essential that these lines are at right angles to assure an even pattern; recheck for accuracy.

Installing the Tiles:
1. For easier installation and better appearance, the border tiles should be as wide as possible and of equal size on both sides of the room. Lay a row of loose tiles along one chalkline from the center to a side wall until no more full tiles can be placed.

2. Measure the space left from the last tile to the wall. If less than half a tile (6″), shift the room center point a half tile in either direction. Snap a new chalkline, parallel with the first, through this new room center point. Be sure the new chalkline still forms a right angle. Repeat this procedure along the other original chalkline and resnap a new chalkline if necessary. Recheck again for accuracy, to be sure the new chalklines form an accurate right angle.

3. After carefully planning the centerlines, you can start installing the tiles. Only remove the backing paper from each tile one at a time, just before putting it in place. The paper is very slippery, so do not stand on it; dispose of each one as you remove it.

4. Start laying tiles at the center of the room, making sure that the first tiles are square with the chalkline. Butt each tile squarely up to the adjoining tile, making sure that the corners meet exactly. Do not slide the tile into place or press down until the tile is positioned correctly. Lay the tiles along this line until no more full tiles will fit. Go back and lay additional rows of full tiles, until one quarter of the room is finished. Repeat with each quarter of the room, until all full tiles are installed.

5. To fit the border tiles, refer to diagram shown here.

Place a loose tile (A) over the closest tile to the wall.

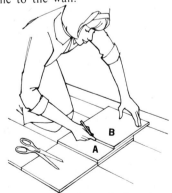

Line it up exactly with the edges of the tile below and with the paper side down. Take another loose tile (B), place it over tile A and slide it to butt against the wall. Mark tile A along the back edge of tile B as shown. Place tile B aside. Transfer your markings to the paper side of tile A by nicking the edges at the mark, turning over the tile and connecting the nicks with a straight-edge. Using heavy shears or utility knife, cut tile A along this line with the paper side up. Make all cuts before removing the backing paper and always cut with the paper side up.

6. To fit tiles around pipes and other obstructions, make a paper pattern first. Place a mark on the top of the pattern and place the pattern over the paper side of the tile, with the mark against the backing paper. Transfer the pattern and cut the tile. If cutting is difficult, warm the tile slightly over a hot plate or in the oven.

7. Replace quarter-round moldings or cove base, if any.

Care and Cleaning: Wait at least 3 days after installing floor tiles before washing them; they must have time to adhere to the subfloor. Scrubbing and frequent washing are not necessary. Regular sweeping or vacuuming, as well as prompt spill removal, maintains the tiles. When you wash, don't flood them with water or use strong detergents, cleaners or waxes containing solvents. Use a sponge mop, squeezing out most of the water before mopping, and give the floor a light rinsing with clean water.

HANGING WALLCOVERING IN EASY STEPS

(page 6)
Wallcoverings offer a quick and easy way to dramatically transform a room. For the best results, just follow these directions.

MATERIALS: Wallcovering (you can choose from stripable wallpaper, fabric-backed vinyl, prepasted wallpaper and pretrimmed wallcoverings in a variety of patterns and colors); yardstick; scissors; stepladder; chalk, string and set of keys (for plumb line); sharp razor-knife; metal edge ruler; seam roller; paste brush and wallcovering paste (if wallcovering is not prepasted); large sponge and bucket; drop cloths; water tray (if using prepasted wallcovering); smoothing brush.

DIRECTIONS:

Determining the Amount of Wall Covering You'll Need:
Measure the width of each wall in feet with yardstick or metal measure, *not* a tape measure. Add these numbers together and multiply this number by the height of the room from ceiling to floor; then divide this number by 30. (If your room is 12'x12'x10'x10', then it would be 44' times 8'=352, divided by 30, or 11¾ rolls.) Subtract ½ roll for each normal-size window and door. This gives you the number of single rolls of wallcovering you will need.

(**Note:** Wallcoverings come in a variety of widths; some of the most common are 20½", 24", 27" and 28". But whatever the width, each roll contains 36 square feet which will cover approximately 30 square feet of wall surface. By dividing the number of square feet in the room by 30, you will have enough wallcovering to match most patterns. If there is a great space between pattern repeats, ask your wallcovering dealer how much more to buy.)

Getting Ready:
• Wash walls in hot water and detergent or ammonia; rinse thoroughly and allow to dry completely.
• Remove electrical outlet coverings.
• Repair any cracks or holes in walls; sand enamel surfaces lightly. Paint trims and any other surfaces not to be covered with wallcovering.
• Trim wallcovering, if not already trimmed, *before pasting.*
• Reroll each roll of wallcovering, inspecting for defects or possible color variations.
• Establish a plumb line on first wall: Attach a string to a plumb bob or a set of keys; rub string with chalk. Attach string to a point near the ceiling that is about 1" less than the width of the wallcovering. Hold the keys taut at baseboard and snap string. This will give you a true vertical line to follow when hanging first strip of wallcovering.
• Measure first strip of wallcovering on wall, adding 4" for adjustments at ceiling and baseboard; carefully cut with scissors.

Preparing Wallcovering Strip:
Using prepasted wallcovering—Fill water tray with lukewarm water and place on drop cloth near wall. Place ladder diagonally in front of tray. Reroll first strip loosely from *bottom to top* with pattern-side in and paste-side out, and cover with water, following manufacturer's directions. Remove strip slowly from tray; bring top of strip to ceiling line.
Using unpasted wallcovering—Prepare wallcovering paste, following label directions, using *cold* water and stirring until paste is lump-free and thin enough to brush on smoothly. Turn wallcovering strips, pattern-side down, onto flat work surface. (You can use the floor, if you first cover the work area with a drop cloth.) Unroll strip and place a book at either end to keep covering from curling. Spread paste evenly on wallcovering with paste brush, starting at center and working to either end with figure 8 strokes. "Book" strip by folding one top edge to center, and *do not crease.* Fold second edge towards center, then fold each edge a second time. Allow to "rest" 3 to 5 minutes for paste to moisten wallcovering evenly.

Hanging Wallcovering:
Place strip, top end at ceiling, overlapping by about 2". Line up right edge of strip with plumb line, so paper will hang evenly. Pat wallcovering into place with open hands, then smooth covering on wall with smoothing brush, removing bubbles by brushing from center toward the edges.

Trim excess wallcovering with razor-knife and metal edge ruler; wipe all paste from covering with sponge and clear water.

Measure second strip of wallcovering, matching pattern, if necessary, and allowing 2" extra on top and bottom; cut and soak or paste strip.

Place second strip so that patterns match, and butt seam without overlapping; smooth with brush; roll seam roller along edge joining to secure; wipe strip with sponge and water. Continue until room is covered, changing water often.

Replace electrical outlet coverings when all walls are covered.

TRACK POT AND PAN HOLDER

(page 9)

MATERIALS: Two 1"x2" pine strips in desired length; four 2½" hexagon bolts; washers; screw nuts; aluminum pot rack hooks (see Buyer's Guide); four 1½" eye hooks.
DIRECTIONS: Drill four ½" holes in pine strips as follows: Make first holes 1½" in from each end; make two more holes which divide the pine strips into three equal sections. Place 2½" hexagon bolts into each of the holes drilled. Place washer and screw nut on the outside of 1"x2". Purchase as many pot rack hooks as you need, keeping in mind that four are needed to hang the rack. Place hooks (hook down) between 1"x2" pine strips. Reverse four hooks at equal distances (hook facing up). Screw four 1½" eye hooks into ceiling to line up with four reversed hooks. Hang from ceiling.

WASHABLE SHIRRED WALLS

(pages 62 and 74)

(**Note:** Also see directions on page 93 for COVERING WALLS WITH FABRIC.) The great thing about these fabric covered walls is that they are hung with Velcro® strips and can be pulled down, then thrown in the washer, and hung back up.
MATERIALS: Sheets or fabric—Determining the amount of wallcovering you'll need: Measure the width of each wall in inches with yardstick or metal measure, *not* a tape measure. Add these numbers together and multiply by the height of the walls, plus

4" for hems; divide by the width of the fabric to be used and then by 36" for number of yards. Or in the case of sheets, see the yardage chart on page 90. (Say that you have a 12' x 10' room that is 8' high to cover. You would add 144" + 120" + 144" + 120" for a total of 528"; then multiply it by 100" for 52,800". Divide this number by the width of the fabric, say 44/45", for a total of 1200" and divide this number by 36" for a total of 33⅓ yards.)

You will need sheets or fabric to equal twice this number. Thread to match; ¾" Velcro® strips to equal twice the wall width measurement (see Buyer's Guide); staple gun.

DIRECTIONS: Seam sheets or fabric as necessary to get one piece with desired dimensions. Turn under ½" on floor and ceiling ends of fabric; turn under 1½" again and stitch hem close to edge. Make gathering stitches with a long machine stitch or a ruffling attachment, ¾" in from ceiling end of fabric, through all thicknesses. Make a second row ¾" in from previous stitching. Repeat for floor end of fabric. Machine-stitch along long edges of one section of Velcro® strips to wrong side of fabric, under rows of gathering stitches. Apply remaining section of Velcro® to walls with a staple gun. (Note: bottom edge of velcro strips should be 1½" away from edge of floor and ceiling to match strips sewn to fabric.)

UPHOLSTERED ROOM

(page 67)

FABRIC-COVERED SCREENS
MATERIALS: ½" interior plywood, two 4'x8' pieces; approximately 10 yds. fabric; 4 butt hinges; staple gun; jig saw or coping saw; #2 common pine, 10 pieces 1"x2".
DIRECTIONS: Cut the ½" interior plywood into 4 pieces, 6'8"x18". Cut 1"x2" to fit around the edges. Lay fabric over each piece of plywood; measure an additional 2" all around. Cut fabric and stretch over plywood, stapling in back. Now cut a piece of fabric to fit the back of each panel. Staple all around edges. Attach hinges about 12" from top and bottom.

FABRIC-COVERED CUBES
MATERIALS (for 2 cubes): ½" interior plywood, 1 sheet of 4'x8'; approximately 5 yds. fabric; staple gun; finishing nails; two 16"x16" pieces of glass.
DIRECTIONS: Cut plywood as follows: 4 pieces 15"x15½"; 4 pieces 15½"x16"; 2 pieces 16"x16". Each cube consists of one 16" square top, *(Continued on page 90.)*

SPRAY-PAINTED DESK

(page 22)

Use an old or unpainted desk for this project. Fill gouges, scratches, etc., with spackling compound, then paint as directed.

MATERIALS: Spackling compound; sandpaper; three cans of spray paint (we used Krylon's Interior/Exterior Spray Enamel in Pastel Aqua #2002, True Blue #1910 and Aqua Turquoise #2008); ¾"-wide and ½"-wide aluminum tape; masking tape; newspapers.
DIRECTIONS: Prepare desk surfaces by filling with spackling compound and sanding smooth. Smooth all surfaces of unfinished material, using very fine grade abrasive sandpaper. Remove all drawers and spray bottom half of each with True Blue paint. Spray Pastel Aqua on top half, including top of drawer front, allowing colors to overlap in a "misty" pattern, as in photo. Let paint dry for at least two hours.

On our desk, the chevrons are 1¾" on the deep drawers and 1¼" on the wider, shallower drawers. To achieve our design, run strips of masking tape from the top corner of drawer to bottom center, and up to other top corner, leaving an opening for chevron to be sprayed. (Wider drawers require two chevrons.) Cover all areas of the drawer front with

PREPARING DESK FOR SPRAY—PAINTED DESIGN

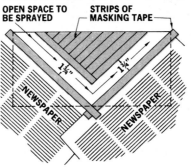

OPEN SPACE TO BE SPRAYED — STRIPS OF MASKING TAPE

masking tape *except* for the chevron strip (see diagram on Preparing Desk for Spray-Painted Design). You can use newspapers for any large areas that are not to be sprayed. Spray the True Blue on the upper portions of the chevrons, stopping at about the horizontal centerline, as in photo. After this dries, spray the bottom portions with Aqua Turquoise.

Remove the taped section in the center of the V; spray lightly with Aqua Turquoise to fill in the center of the V approximately halfway between the top and centerline, as in photo, letting the spray feather out as shown.

Now take the aluminum tape (¾" for the deep drawers and ½" for the

shallow drawers) and run it along the top edge of the chevron, overlapping the top edge and inside of the drawer about 2". Where the two pieces of tape meet in the bottom center of the V, slice down between them vertically with a razor blade, removing the overlapping edges.

When all the drawers are finished, spray-paint the rest of the desk, using True Blue up to the centerline of the top drawer. Spray the Pastel Aqua on the upper portion from where the dark color left off. Use at least two coats on the top to protect it from damage. Three coats are preferable, with adequate drying time (two hours) between each coat.

SPRAY-PAINTED PICTURE FRAME

(page 22)

Highlight your favorite photo with an original picture frame. You can use the design shown, or make your own with other colors and patterns.
MATERIALS: Picture-frame glass (ours is 11"x14"); spray paint (we used Krylon's Interior/Exterior Spray Enamel in True Blue #1910, Banner Red #2108, School Bus Yellow #1809 and Bright Silver #1401); 11"x14" cardboard back with easel; masking tape; crayon; "Braquettes" for holding glass and back together.
DIRECTIONS: First determine exactly where you want the photo to be placed, then block off that area with masking tape on one side of the glass. On the same side, draw guidelines in crayon for tape in the shapes of our silver line designs (see photo). On reverse side of glass, place masking tape over guidelines. Now begin spraying over tape, from the bottom up. True Blue was used about halfway up in our example, and allowed to dry. The next one-quarter of the glass was sprayed with Banner Red, allowing the color to feather out, or mist over, the color below. The last color covers the remainder of the glass, also misting onto the color below. Allow ample drying time between each color. Now remove the masking tape used for the lines, and spray with the silver paint. Remove the rest of the masking tape, remove crayon with damp cloth and tape the photo to the back of the glass, so that it shows through the unpainted center. If the right size back cardboard and easel are not available, you can make your own out of heavy cardboard, stapling the easel to the back section. The glass and back are held together with the Braquette corners. To change the photo, remove the Braquettes, untape the photo and insert the new one.

(page 23)

Directions 'are given for all lamps shown and include a light socket assembly diagram (page 107) to which you can refer as you complete each lamp. For information on buying lamp parts, see Buyer's Guide or try your local hardware store.

MAILING TUBE LAMP

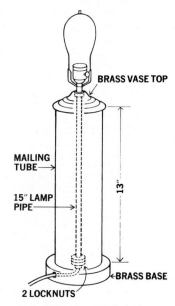

BRASS VASE TOP

MAILING TUBE

15" LAMP PIPE

13"

BRASS BASE

2 LOCKNUTS

MAILING TUBE LAMP

MATERIALS: 4½" x 13" mailing tube; decorative wrapping paper; 4½" spun brass vase top; 6" spun brass base; 15" brass straight lamp pipe; 3 locknuts; light socket and harp; 8' UL approved lamp cord; 6" round felt piece; 13" round lamp shade; spray adhesive.

DIRECTIONS: Cut decorative wrapping paper to cover outside of mailing tube. Coat paper with spray adhesive and wrap around tube to cover completely. Connect lamp pipe to brass base using 2 locknuts, as shown in Mailing Tube Lamp diagram. Coat brass bottom with spray adhesive; press felt pad into place. Next place mailing tube over pipe and place brass vase top over tube; secure with locknut. Insert lamp cord through brass base and up through pipe; attach harp to pipe; connect lamp pipe to socket base with locknut. Connect wire to screw terminals; complete socket assembly. Place shade on.

PENNSYLVANIA DUTCH PAINTED BOX LAMP

MATERIALS: 2½ ft. of ½" x 9" pine board (for box); ¾" pine board, 7" x 9½" (for base); one ¾" x 2½" x 6" piece of wood (lamp pipe support);

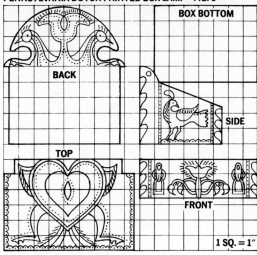

BOX BOTTOM

BACK

SIDE

TOP

FRONT

1 SQ. = 1"

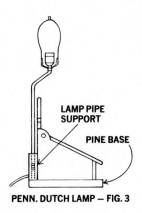

LAMP PIPE SUPPORT

PINE BASE

PENN. DUTCH LAMP — FIG. 3

12" bent arm lamp pipe; 1 lamp socket and harp; 1 locknut; 8' UL approved lamp cord; 1 tube each acrylic paint in yellow oxide, ultramarine blue, Indian red, chrome green, and white; 7" x 9½" felt pad; 13" x 8½" lamp shade; coping saw or electric jigsaw, electric or hand drill with ⅜" drill bit; sandpaper; white wood glue; paint brushes; small nails; two 1" wood screws.

DIRECTIONS: Following directions on page 37, but using tracing paper, enlarge and cut out patterns in Fig. 1 of Pennsylvania Dutch Lamp diagram; trace the outline of the back, top, bottom, side and front shapes onto pine board; cut out parts with coping saw or electric jigsaw. Sand all edges smooth; assemble sides back and bottom, using glue and small nails; hinge top to sides with 1" wood screws placed ¾" in from edge of sides into top piece. Paint box, base and

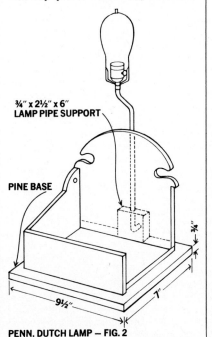

¾" x 2½" x 6"
LAMP PIPE SUPPORT

PINE BASE

9½"

7"

¾"

PENN. DUTCH LAMP — FIG. 2

lamp pipe support with yellow oxide; allow to dry completely. Smudge back of each traced design with pencil. Lay tracing paper on box; right-side up, and go over the designs once again in pencil. The imprint will be left on the box. Now, following photo, paint in designs, working one color at a time. (The small white dots are made by using the wooden end of a small paintbrush.) Drill a hole for pipe through top of ¾"x2½"x6" lamp pipe support with ⅜" drill bit, as shown in Fig. 2. Drill a second hole at back to intersect with top hole for cord outlet. Glue and nail lamp pipe support to pine base in back of box (see Fig. 3). Insert wire through cord outlet and up through pipe; insert pipe into support as shown. Attach harp to pipe; connect lamp pipe to socket base with locknut; connect wire to screw terminals; complete socket assembly. Glue felt to bottom of base; glue box to base. Place shade on lamp.

TABBY CAT LAMP

MATERIALS: Muslin Tabby Cat pattern #3634 (see Buyer's Guide); polyester fiberfill; 1½" x 5" x 9" pine base; 15" brass plated straight lamp pipe; 1 locknut; 8' UL approved lamp cord; light socket and harp; 21" x 19" rative fabric; 13" x 8½" lamp shade; spray adhesive; razor blade; electric or hand drill with ⅜" bit.

DIRECTIONS: Cut out cat pattern; sew and stuff with fiberfill, following kit directions. Drill a 1" hole through the top center of pine base with ⅜" drill bit; drill a second hole in back of base to intersect with top hole for cord outlet. Coat top of pine base with spray adhesive; center on fabric; coat sides of wood with adhesive; press fabric over; coat underside with adhesive and cover with fabric. Cut hole in material with razor blade to expose hole for lamp pipe. Open a ½"

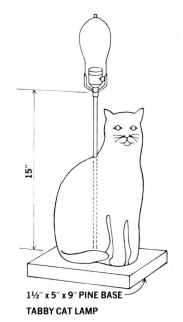

15″

1½″ x 5″ x 9″ PINE BASE

TABBY CAT LAMP

seam on cat's back at top and bottom (see Tabby Cat Lamp diagram). Insert lamp pipe through cat and fiberfill. Slip stitch seams closed around pipe. Insert lamp cord through base and up through lamp pipe. Insert pipe into base; attach harp to pipe; connect pipe to socket base with locknut; connect wire to screw terminals; complete socket assembly. Place shade on lamp. (You can find shades at your local five and ten cent store.)

shade; coping saw or electric jigsaw; electric or hand drill with ⅜″ drill bit; pocket knife; sandpaper; fine steel wool; paintbrush; spray adhesive.

DIRECTIONS: Following directions on page 37, enlarge and cut out pattern in Fig. 1 of Whale Weathervane Lamp diagram; trace onto pine board; cut out with coping saw or electric jigsaw. Sand all edges smooth; chisel out whale's eye, ear, mouth, fins and tail with pocket knife. Drill hole through whale and wooden ball with ⅜″ drill bit, as shown in Fig. 2. Drill a 2″ deep hole into pine base from right of center at top and a second hole at side to intersect with top hole for cord outlet, as shown. Paint whale, base and wooden ball with red paint; allow to dry; paint over with coat of black paint; allow to dry. For a weathered look, rub wood with steel wool until parts of red paint and raw wood start to show through black paint. Coat bottom of base with spray adhesive and press felt piece into place. Insert lamp pipe through whale and wooden ball; thread lamp cord through hole in base and up through lamp pipe. Insert pipe into wood base. Attach harp to pipe; connect pipe to socket base with locknut; connect wire to screw terminals; complete socket assembly. Place shade on lamp.

DIRECTIONS: Starting at the top, drill hole through the center of wooden base to within 1″ of bottom with ⅜″ drill bit. (A doweling jig can be helpful since it will enable you to drill straight holes, if you don't have access to a drill press. They can be purchased for about $12 at a hardware store.) Drill a second hole at back of base bottom to meet center hole for cord outlet as shown in Wood Spindle Lamp diagram. Coat bottom

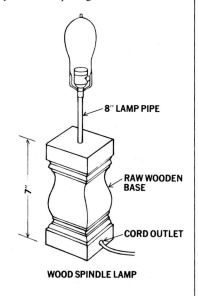

8″ LAMP PIPE

RAW WOODEN BASE

7″

CORD OUTLET

WOOD SPINDLE LAMP

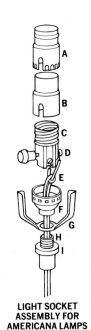

A. OUTER METAL SHEATH

B. CARDBOARD INSULATION

C. SOCKET WITH SCREW TERMINALS

D. SCREW TERMINALS WITH LAMP WIRE CONNECTED

E. UL APPROVED LAMP CORD

F. SOCKET BASE

G. DETACHABLE HARP BASE

H. THREADED END OF LAMP PIPE

I. LOCKNUT

LIGHT SOCKET ASSEMBLY FOR AMERICANA LAMPS

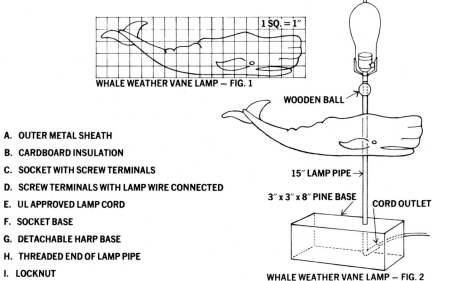

1 SQ. = 1″

WHALE WEATHER VANE LAMP — FIG. 1

WOODEN BALL

15″ LAMP PIPE

3″ x 3″ x 8″ PINE BASE

CORD OUTLET

WHALE WEATHER VANE LAMP — FIG. 2

WHALE WEATHER VANE LAMP

MATERIALS: ¾″ x 5″ x 18″ pine board; 3″ x 3″ x 8″ pine base; 1″ wooden ball; 15″ brass plated straight lamp pipe; 1 locknut; 1 lamp socket and harp; 8′ UL approved lamp cord; 1 tube each red and black acrylic paint; 3″ x 5″ felt pad; 13″ x 8½″ lamp

WOOD SPINDLE LAMP

MATERIALS: 7″ decorative raw wooden base (available at lumber yards); 8″ straight lamp pipe; 1 locknut; 8′ UL approved lamp cord; light socket and harp; 9″ lamp shade; 4″ square felt pad; electric drill with ⅜″ drill bit; spray adhesive.

of base with spray adhesive and center felt piece in place. Insert wire through base and into lamp pipe. Insert pipe into wood base; attach harp to pipe; connect lamp pipe to socket base with locknut. Connect wire to screw terminals; complete socket assembly. Place shade on lamp.

(Continued from page 18)
required width without a seam down the center of the table.) Fold prepared cloth or sheet, right sides together, in half, lengthwise, then in half, crosswise, to make a rectangle 4 layers thick. Using non-stretchy cord to serve as a compass, knot one end and pin to center corner of fabric. Tie a pencil to other end of string. Length should be half of diameter of table, plus distance to floor, plus ½". (With our table, 15" + 28" + ½" = 43½".) Mark the outer edge of cloth with pencil; cut with sharp scissors. Stitch a ½" hem around cloth; press.

DECORATING DOLLARS
(Continued from page 20)
chairs and try to tip them over. They won't rock if the legs are anchored well. Place your hands on a table and try rocking it; if it wobbles, it's poorly constructed. Well made furniture should be braced with tightly screwed-on wooden blocks.

Comfort is one of the most important things to consider, especially when buying upholstered furniture. To test a piece for comfort and durability, sit on it and bounce up and down a few times. The piece should not creak, and should provide good back support. If it's a sofa you're checking out, have someone else test it along with you. Two or more people should be able to sit comfortably.

Next, feel the upholstery to be sure it's well padded and without lumps. You shouldn't be able to feel the framework through the upholstery; if you do, there isn't enough padding between the fabric and the framework. To judge whether a sofa will endure heavy wear, lift one corner; the other should remain on the floor with no movement or shifting. Quality sofas will be glued and joined with double-doweled joints and reinforced with block corners.

Now run your hand under the upholstered piece—you should feel webbing laced together and covered with burlap or mesh. Good webbing is wide and closely woven and helps support the springs in upholstered furniture. Further indications of quality are reversible cushions, a self-covered deck under the cushions and tufting sturdily held by buttons sewn through the filling. Other things to look for are straight seams, straight welting and a snug fit of all the cushions together. The contents of the cushions are important, too. Manufacturers are required by law to specify contents and proportions of filling mixture, so ask your salesman to show you a sample of the materials used.

Checks for fabrics: The patterns should be well matched throughout the entire piece, and the material used

should be non-flammable. Pull hard at the fabric in several directions—if the yarn slips or separates, there's probably a weakness in the fabric's construction. To assure yourself of a tightly woven fabric, hold a swatch of it up to a lamp—no light should filter through. Also scratch a printed fabric with your fingernail. If color comes off, it's of poor quality.

Finally, consider the care a piece of furniture will require once it's in your home. Ask the salesman questions about fabric composition and wood finishes to be sure you're not buying something that's going to be difficult to maintain. And know exactly what your guarantees offer in the way of satisfaction for your investment. ∎

FURNITURE CARE
(Continued from page 19)
you've filled. Then rub down with rottenstone and oil solution.

Water Rings—There are several ways you can try removing water marks from furniture. One method is applying a paste wax with 3/0 steel wool, working with the grain of wood, then polishing. You can also apply a rottenstone and oil treatment or rub the spot lightly with a soft cloth moistened with camphorated oil and wipe immediately with a clean cloth. Another method is to cover the mar with a clean, thick blotter and press with a warm, *not* hot, iron until it disappears.

Paint Stains—If the paint is an oil-based one and the stain is still fresh, you can remove it with a slightly moistened cloth and liquid wax. For old paint stains, cover the area with linseed oil, letting it stand until the paint becomes soft. Then wipe with more linseed oil.

White Marks Caused by Heat—These are usually difficult to repair, but a camphorated oil treatment may help. Rub the spot lightly with a lint-free cloth moistened with the oil and then wipe clean with another cloth. You might also try the rottenstone and oil technique.

CREDITS

HOW TO ENLARGE DESIGNS

If the design is not already marked off in squares, make a tracing of it. Next, mark the tracing off in squares; for a small design, make squares ¼"; for larger designs, use ½", 1" or 2" squares. Decide the size of your enlargement; on another sheet of tracing paper, mark off the same number of squares that are on the design or original tracing. Remember that to make your design six times larger than the original design, each new square must be six times larger than the original. Carefully copy the outline from your original tracing to the new one, square by square. Use dressmaker's carbon and a tracing wheel to transfer the design to the material you're decorating.

Graphic hall by designer Allen Scruggs is outlined in several colors of Fuller O'Brien paint. A soft blue carpet by Galaxy and inexpensive baskets hung on walls and over a light fixture add new textures.

FIRST IMPRESSIONS

Wallcovering changes the same hall into a traditional and slightly more formal area. The wall below the chair rail is painted in order to break up what could be an overpowering use of wallcovering in such a small space.

Simple changes in an entrance hall, like colorful wallcovering or a collection of your favorite accessories, can introduce your decorating taste and set the style for the rest of your home.

COLORFUL WALLCOVERING
and plush carpeting on the stairs add softness and light to a once dark Victorian hallway. The low ledge here is an ideal spot to show off a personal collection of decorative objects, such as these paperweights.

CREATE A TOTAL LOOK
with one motif used throughout a small entrance hall. The pineapple, a traditional symbol of hospitality, says welcome on this stencil-like wallcovering. A custom-made stained glass window continues the pattern on the door.

Pierced brass lamp, imported from India, was once a water jug. Topped with a simple shade, it shows how an interesting container can be converted into a handsome accessory.

This is a time of numerous trends and design styles. Yet they all point to one basic conclusion: When in doubt, let your own personal taste rule. With this point in mind, we offer here a sampling of furniture designs for you to choose from to achieve a look all your own.

NEW FOR YOU

CLASSIC LINES

on a Chinese-influenced chest enable it to mix with any style decor. The dark wood and metal details reminiscent of Chinese design are always in popularity.

IMPORTED
Italian chair is acero and walnut inlay
veneer on beechwood, forming a very
unique graphic pattern.

TURN-OF-THE-CENTURY
influence is apparent in a stylish love seat with interesting wood turnings. A mixture of contemporary
fabrics in upholstery and throw pillows brings the total look very up-to-date.

POTTERY JUG

forms the base and a pleated print fabric makes the shade of this handsome lamp. It adds a charming, country look to any decor.

HIGH-STYLED

ottoman takes on a new shape. Fabric covering is softly pleated and banded in the middle, making this a decorative piece, but at the same time, very practical seating.

43

EXPANDABLE
dining table is
ideal for apartment
living or wherever
small dining space
is a problem.
Bamboo-like details
give it a more casual
look that blends
well with both
modern and
traditional interiors.

UNUSUAL CURVES
on a pleated
fabric shade blend
well with the soft
shape and delicate
colors of this
Chinese-influenced
lamp. It's suited
for more formal and
traditional interiors.

TRADITIONAL
lamp with brass trim was
once used with candles. Today it offers
good lighting for a side table or desk.

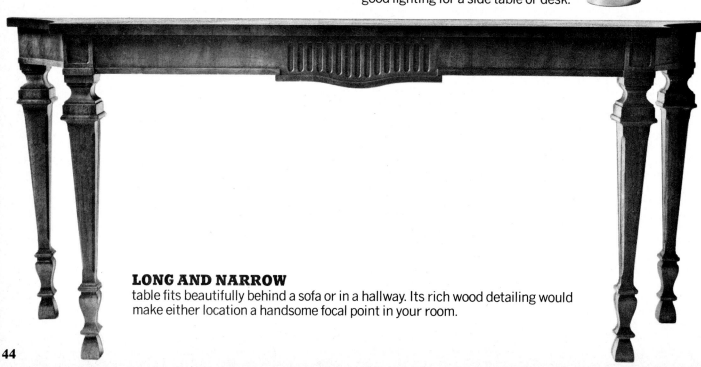

LONG AND NARROW
table fits beautifully behind a sofa or in a hallway. Its rich wood detailing would
make either location a handsome focal point in your room.

PUFFY SIDE CHAIR features Parsons legs and design lines reminiscent of the 1930's. Flame stitch pattern and plump look would lend a soft touch to either living room or bedroom.

TINY LAMP with traditional details and an interesting marbleized lamp shade is small enough to fit on a bookcase shelf. Watch for these small lamps to grow in popularity.

FAN LAMP
is lit from behind for an unusual and decorative effect. Looks smashing with both modern and Oriental decors.

TEA TABLE
features Chinese-inspired styling. It has handsome wood side panels that slip out to hold serving pieces or accessories.

SHELL SHAPED brass floor lamp takes the look of a pharmacy lamp one step further. It's a terrific space-saver and mixes well with both modern and traditional decors.

DRIFTWOOD FINISH and a washable canvas seat cushion make this a very practical, not to mention comfortable, chair to live with. Perfect for today's casual look.

SHINY CERAMIC LAMP has a broad base and a paper pleated shade that sheds plenty of light on the subject. Its graceful lines make it stylish enough for any room.

OUTDOOR CHAIR

comes indoors for a strictly informal setting. Natural finish and slatted seat add to its casual look. Adjustable for sitting or reclining.

BAMBOO MOTIF

lamp has a natural appeal that works well with today's informal settings. Its neutral tones make it an easy mixer with almost any color scheme.

MODULAR SEATING

provides the flexibility needed for today's movable society. These units look smart when used either singly or grouped together in a variety of shapes.

RATTAN topped end table is trimmed with chrome for a sleek and distinctly modern look. Its unusual top lends an easy, casual look to living room or den.

SHINY BRASS candlestick lamp is a traditional design that still maintains its ability to blend well with almost any decorating style. Its classic lines make it a handsome accessory in almost any room.

1930's INSPIRED
love seat features plump, rounded lines and a smart-looking style all its own. Now, the look has been updated with rich-looking velvet upholstery for an added touch of luxury.

SOFT-LINE
puffy side chairs show the influence of 1930's styling in their plump, rounded lines. They're the ultimate in comfy seating.

UPDATED
version of the old kerosene lamp looks terrific in silver and milk glass.

PORTABLE BAR
is as handsome opened as it is closed. It has a mirrored top and built-in ice bucket, with plenty of enclosed storage space down below.

NATURAL OAK
drop-leaf dining table neatly folds to a
narrow size—can even be put in a hallway. Sides flip up
conveniently and offer room enough to serve a crowd.

CONTEMPORARY
floor lamp is a flexible space-saver.
Its wide-based shade makes it an ideal reading
lamp next to sofa or bed.

**SLING
CHAIR**
with leather
seat and
chrome frame
has an
interesting
modern look.
Its compact
size and
sleek look
make it
a terrific choice
for apartment
living at dining
table or desk.

LOUIS XV CHAIR

has a natural finish on fruitwood and is richly upholstered in tabasco-colored cotton velvet. Its graceful lines blend well with traditional interiors.

BRASS TRIMMED TABLE

has a decorative scalloped edge on a glass top, giving it a more formal look. It would make an excellent coffee table in the living room or study, and is a versatile enough design to blend with many settings.

TUB CHAIRS

used alone or in pairs, make versatile contemporary mixers. Use them for comfy seating in living room, bedroom, family room or den.

GINGER JAR
lamp has a base that is delicately strewn with flowers and is topped with a softly-pleated shade. It works best in traditional settings.

COUNTRY FRENCH
chair has a casual, yet elegant, charm with its carved wood designs on a painted finish, and comfortable fabric seat cushion. Makes an excellent dining chair or side chair.

POTTERY BASE
lamp has a simplicity of design which allows it to mingle comfortably with almost any style interior.

TRADITIONAL
dining chair with an interesting back and softly-padded seat, offers comfortable seating in a variety of decors.

THE HITCHCOCK CHAIR
first came to popularity in early 19th century America and still retains its appeal today. Its woven rush seat and painted-design frame are part of its charm.

REGENCY CHAIR
is delicately designed and trimmed in gold with contemporary-look upholstery. Blends well with more formal settings and makes an elegant accent piece.

FRETWORK DESIGN
dining chair has a handsome beechwood frame with a mahogany finish. Chinese-influenced style and plush beige velvet cushion lend it to more formal decors.

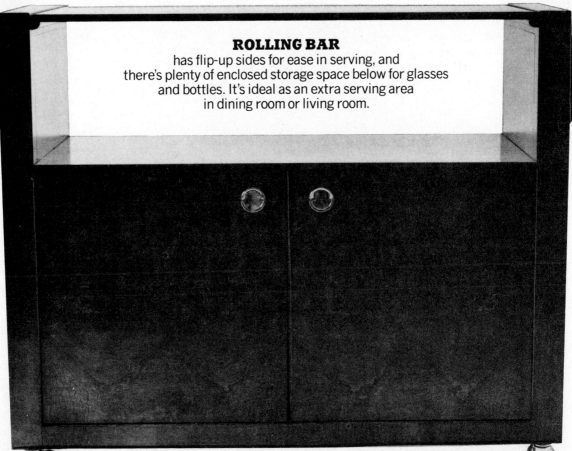

ROLLING BAR
has flip-up sides for ease in serving, and there's plenty of enclosed storage space below for glasses and bottles. It's ideal as an extra serving area in dining room or living room.

GLASS-TOP TABLE

has a rattan border insert for an extra handsome touch. Its sleek chrome and glass styling makes it an excellent mixer with contemporary and modern decors. Perfect for a hallway or behind a sofa.

CONTEMPORARY SWIVEL LAMP

is trimmed with brass and has a natural-look rattan base; softly-pleated shade gives it a casual look. It makes a super reading lamp and would look great on desk or night table.

TABLES OF CONTENTS

Quickly change the look of a room by
simply setting the table! A Tiffany lamp is the
focal point and inspiration for this
coordinated table setting of Franciscan China.

ORIENTAL SETTING

The exotic look of this dining room designed by Meredith White for Bloomingdale's, is far less expensive to achieve than you might imagine. The china and matching accessories are current design pieces with the look of valuable Oriental antiques. Rattan trays, used instead of place mats, pick up the border motif of the table and, along with the rattan furniture, lend an informal, yet elegant, look to this dining room area.

VICTORIAN ELEGANCE

A romantic, elegant mood is created against a background of refinished second-hand furniture and painted mantel. The Royal Copenhagen china pattern picks up the room's color scheme and is further enhanced by matching napkins and candles.

59

**EARLY
AMERICAN
DINING ROOM**
has an inviting
quality that is
further enhanced
by a fabric-covered
window wall. The
Schumacher fabric
adds warmth and
drama to the setting
and nicely
complements the
modern Wedgwood
china on the table.
Though it looks
delicate, the china
is durable enough
to go in the
dishwasher, and
serving pieces go
from oven to table.

**PERSONALIZE
THE ROOM**
with an interesting and colorful
assortment of accessories displayed on
an open shelf. The combination of
colors and textures shown here adds
a rich highlight to the setting.

ACCENTUATE THE POSITIVE
Modern furnishings accentuate the architectural details of this dining room. Red accents on wall and table add warmth to the setting. The strawberry poster is actually a piece of colorful fabric stretched over a wooden frame.

FABRIC COVER-UP
Cover walls with the same fabric as your tablecloth. Designer Everett Brown hung shirred fabric using Velcro tape for easy maintenance.

For project how-to's, see index on page 89.

BAY WINDOW

brings the outdoors in by functioning as a mini greenhouse for plants. Continue the natural theme indoors with an inexpensive sisal rug and colorful floral centerpiece. The Minton china is a permanent bouquet of flowers on leaf green mats.

COUNTRY DINING has an ease and informality reflected in this room designed by Everett Brown. A handsome wood table shows off its natural beauty minus a heavy tablecloth, and reflects the clean, uncluttered look of the windows, decorated with pots of fresh flowers.

THE HISTORICAL APPROACH
A traditional fabric seemed most appropriate for this 18th Century American bedroom. So Everett Brown chose one with a history—and currently available—to drape the four-poster and windows.

UPHOLSTERED SOFTNESS
Designer Allen Scruggs didn't confine Herculon's upholstery fabrics to just chairs and sofas. He also wrapped them around screens, cubes and pillows for a custom coordinated look. Two cubes, topped with glass and set at angles, form an unusual coffee table; a plant or sculpture stand uses the same technique. Cover a screen for more textural variety.

QUICK ROOM CHANGES

You needn't knock down walls or invest lots of time and money to redo a room. Fabric, paint and a few accessories can work wonders.

For project how-to's, see index on page 89.

PAINT YOUR BEDROOM WITH SHEETS

Sheets provide instant coordination when used as the basis of a room's decor. They're easy to maintain, economical to use and come in a wide variety of styles to suit any mood. Sheer romance inspired designer Douglas Myers to choose these Pacific Home Products Fortrel/cotton sheets in Pablo Picasso's "Hands and Flowers" motif. Pure white with delicate, yet dramatic, splashes of color, this pattern lends itself beautifully to the many simple projects shown. Begin by covering the bed with sheets and matching comforter. Using wide sheets, sew flouncy floor-to-ceiling curtains and a ruffled tablecloth. Continue with an assortment of pillows, covered boxes —even a lamp shade! Beribboned window shade adds another light touch to the romance of the room. To balance the busy pattern, use a solid color carpet; this gold one is of easy-care Fortron 50 by Cabin Crafts. Wicker furniture enhances the room's springtime mood. Check your attic or local thrift shop for old pieces; a few coats of light paint will make them fresh and interesting again. While you're hunting for used furniture, choose some attractive antique collectibles; they personalize a room and give it character. An array of colorful potted plants completes the soft decor with flair.

For project how-to's, see index on page 89.

REDRESS A ROOM

with colorful fabrics for a fresh, new look. An overall feeling of unity is achieved when odd pieces of furniture are covered with a striking mixture of patterns in fabrics by Riverdale. And Scotchgard® Fabric Protector makes the look as practical as it is fashionable. After sofa, love seat and chair are slipcovered in coordinated fabrics, the mix-and-match look is carried one step further with the draped table and harem pillows. An old parsons table is spray-painted, picking up one of the colors in the floral sofa fabric. Next, an easy-maintenance area rug with contrasting border was custom-made by piecing together two different sections of Mohawk's Graceful Way carpet. Our method for making the area rug avoids the difficulty of mitered corners and allows you to purchase the smallest amount of carpet possible. Scotchgard® Carpet Protector keeps it looking its best. Finally, the personal touch is added with a selection of colorful accessories.

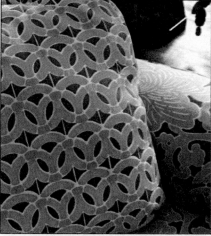

For project how-to's, see index on page 89.

BLACK AND WHITE
give a sleek look to this sophisticated setting of Kroehler Furniture designed by Albert Etienne Pensis of W. & J. Sloane. Mirrored touches complete the look.

WASHABLE WALLCOVERING
by Stauffer Chemical picks up the bright green of the Milliken rug in Anso fibers. Vivid colors make this room a little girl's delight.

COMBINE TWO SHEET PATTERNS
from Bibb on bed, window and table. No need to worry about soiling—they're easy-care Fortrel/cotton. Take the coordinated look one step further and cover lamp shade and picture frame with leftover fabric.

STRETCH YOUR SPACE
by coordinating a bedroom around an exercise area. Armstrong carpet squares and floor tiles, laid in a geometric pattern, let you separate each area and are a cinch to install. Notice how the mirrored wall expands space.

For project how-to's, see index on page 89.

THE COORDINATED LOOK OF SHEETS
Decorate dramatically, using just one pattern of sheets. The Wamsutta bedspread is ready-made; other items—such as shirred fabric walls and fabric-lined shades—are easy to make. Only the love seat requires a bit more sewing skill.

PLAID/PATCHWORK
combination lends a country touch to a room. Cannon Mills' plaid sheets, by designer Sarina Mascheroni, make splendid café curtains, window seat cushions and table cloths. The bedspread comes ready-made. Rocking chair completes the country look.

For project how-to's, see index on page 89.

NATURE'S BEST
Natural materials mix together quietly with limited effort on your part. Combine rattan chairs with slatted blinds, baskets and a sisal rug for a muted effect. Lots of healthy plants and vibrant pillows add splashes of color.

FLOWERED FABRIC-COVERED

walls provide the background pattern for this elegant bedroom. Rich yellow material hangs in pleats from the

canopy, contrasting with the dark wood frame and night table. The two-tone sheet mixture is a simple sewing idea; you might also try using coordinated prints or a print-solid combination.

PICK A BOLD COUNTRY PRINT

and use it throughout a room for a cozy, yet polished look. In this dining room by Mary Salvo of B. Altman and Co., the fabric covers part of the wall and is also used to make curtains and a window seat cushion. (Window seats are easy to construct and look splendid when built into bay windows.) Pillow and lower wall colors echo those in the fabric. Hitchcock table and chairs emphasize the mood.

For project how-to's, see index on page 89.

CREATING INTEREST

in a room that lacks charm takes some simple coordination. This dining room was a boxy, unimaginative space, without a trace of color or architectural interest. By painting the molding around ceiling and chair rail a bright orange, the stage was set for fabric and furniture coordination. Two Waverly fabrics are used imaginatively to set the color scheme. One fabric covers the walls from chair rail to floor, while a patchwork print fabric in coordinating colors is made into draperies. Leftover fabric continues the coordinated look in place mats and lamp shades. Notice how the early American furniture by Pennsylvania House is further enhanced by the charming accessories displayed in the china cabinet and on the buffet.

COMFORTABLE AMERICANA
Easy-to-care-for fabrics, as appealing as they are serviceable, add new charm to older furnishings. Wall-to-wall bookshelves, painted a handsome color, can become the main highlight in a room. Wall trim is painted the same color for a pulled-together look.

PURE ROMANCE
in a room that's easy to put together and maintain. Turn-of-the-century cupboards and oak chairs can be bought in antique or second-hand shops, although new versions are currently being made by furniture manufacturers. Curtains and table runners can go right in the washing machine.

SOUTHWEST INFORMALITY
means an accent on natural elements and American crafts. Here, a unique collection of authentic American Indian basketry and pottery is simply displayed amidst earthy colors and natural textures. Lots of greenery emphasize the total look.

PRETTY YET PRACTICAL
This romantic dining room takes full advantage of washable fabrics and wallcoverings. The floral print wallcovering by Wall-Tex is creatively framed with store-bought wood moldings.

A SOFT COMBINATION
of fabrics in off-beat, warm colors makes this room designed by Meredith White of Bloomingdale's a very inviting setting. Mixing patterns can create stylish interiors if you remember to keep the patterns in the same color range.

DECORATING WITH CRAFTS

Accessorizing a room with crafts you make yourself is what being your own home decorator is all about. Our Patchwork Puff Quilt (opposite), designed by Shirley Botsford for Coats & Clark, will add a warm note to a country casual bedroom. In this section are many more projects that can add a personal touch to every room in your home.

For project how-to's, see index on page 89.

1-6

Romantic pillows, so soft and pretty, are easy to sew with the help of Simplicity patterns. Heart-shaped or ruffled, they accessorize a room stylishly. And for a truly personalized look, spell out your name in pillows!

7-10

Super planters add a touch of Americana to any setting. From top to bottom: Knife Box is decorated with Pennsylvania Dutch designs in acrylics; Fabric-Covered Planter shows off pretty postcards; Planter Chest is printed with a sponge design in acrylics; Shaker Candlestick Holder is a traditional design converted into a planter. Designed by Bruce Murphy for 3M.

11

Simple ruffles made from fabric scraps are attached to a dime store mirror with Wilhold Glue. It's a vision of romantic decorating for any room in the house.

12-14

Give your table a coordinated and elegant look with lace place mats and matching napkins and napkin rings. All are simple projects to make using Simplicity patterns and no-fuss lace fabrics.

15-17

Three inexpensive and very different baskets are given a colorful touch by designer Kathy Moore. They're all done with Krylon spray paint and stencils you make yourself. It's easy to give any room a natural look.

18-19

Stylish containers are actually an inexpensive glass bowl covered with felt cut-outs, and a coffee can wrapped in colorful yarn. Both are designed by Kathy Moore for 3M.

20-21

Frame an inexpensive mirror with an art deco design that's custom-colored for your interior. Mat board is glued in layers to create this modern design in soft natural colors. A picture frame is upholstered in two different floral prints for a unique look. Both designs by Kathy Moore for Wilhold Glue.

22

Fabric Puff Baskets are inexpensive straw baskets that have been lightly stuffed with fiberfill and wrapped in a charming print fabric. Designed by the 3M company.

23

Give any room an elegant, romantic look with lace curtains and coordinated tablecloth and pillows. With the help of Simplicity patterns, this lacy setting is as easy as it is charming.

1-6

7-10

For project how-to's, see index on page 89.

11

12-14

15-17

18-19

20-21

22

23

24-25

26-28

29

30

31-32

33

24-25

Our colorful appliquéd quilt and matching pillows are Lancaster Rose, an original Fab.U.Print design. And the Fab.U.Print design paper plus our how-to's make it easier than you think to give your bedroom the coordinated look that's so popular today.

26-28

Three inexpensive natural wood folding chairs are given dynamic-looking graphic designs using a small amount of time and money. Choose your favorite design and, with pencil and tape, mark a pattern directly on the chair. Krylon spray paint adds the color and aluminum tape gives them finishing touches. All were designed by Peter Davis.

29

A second-hand chair purchased in a thrift shop is rejuvenated with a few simple tricks. The chair was a sorry sight, but with a few coats of Fuller O'Brien paint, the dull, scarred wood took on new life. Simple cushions in a tiny floral print fabric add the finishing touches. Designed by Douglas Myers.

30

An unpainted chest becomes a circus when it's stenciled with a parade of colorful elephants!

Designed by Jennifer for Hunt Manufacturing Co.

31-32

Patchwork chicken and rooster are appliquéd on pillows and a frilly calico ruffle is added for good measure. Sew more than one for a country fresh look. Designed by Michelle and Danielle Koenig and inspired by their mother, Marlene.

33

Natural Bean Lamp sheds an interesting light on a country casual kitchen. A standard photographer's reflector lamp shade is covered in a free-form pattern of beans and seeds secured with glue. Designed by Kathy Moore for the 3M Company.

34-39

Accessories in vibrant colors give character to a neutral color scheme. Lamp shade, table coverlet, leaf and flower pillows are all easy batik crafts requiring just one waxing and one dyeing. Designed by Debbie Durham for Rit Dye.

40

Our flowering grow chart makes a fun, decorative addition to a child's room and will be used for many years to come. The boldly colored design is made of inexpensive Phun Phelt which is cut out using patterns we provide and then simply glued to the background piece. It couldn't be easier! Designed for us by Constance Spates.

For project how-to's, see index on page 89.

41-43

More patchwork appliquéd pillows for giving a country casual feeling to any room, quickly and quite inexpensively.

44

All-in-one record table will really put some order in your life. Record albums stand upright in neat compartments and natural wood shelves hold receiver and turntable. There's even room for a tape deck! Designed for us by René Velez.

45

This handsome parquet table seats six comfortably and costs only a fraction of the price of a store-bought table. It's an easy project to make since the lumber can be pre-cut and Hartco's handsome parquet floor tiles form the table top. Classic lines make this table an easy mixer with traditional and modern decors.

46

Add a custom look to your bathroom with one easy project—a wooden toilet paper holder. Paint it to match the room's color scheme or leave it natural for a rustic look. Designed by Clancy De Roe.

47

Arched Mirror has an unusual raised design formed with modeling paste and painted in soft seascape colors. Made with inexpensive materials, it looks lovely on vanity or dresser. Designed by Barbara Wrenn.

48

Folding indoor/outdoor sling chair by Samsonite takes on a whole new look with a bright blue needle-point posy. The sling material is the working surface for the needlepoint project. Designed by Karen Clark Hagaman.

49

What child wouldn't enjoy a Village Floor Game for his room? Painted in bold colors, kids can play with cars, trucks or blocks on a village layout. And when not in use, it makes a terrific wall decoration. Designed by Barbara Wrenn.

50-53

All-over rose design inspired by Sunworthy's wallcovering, is carried throughout the room with a fabric screen printing method. The stencil is printed on pillows, fabric, deacon's bench and even the rug. Designed by Jennifer for Hunt Manufacturing Co.

54

Wool Stitchery Bouquet is a gorgeous burst of color using a variety of needlepoint stitches in 100% wool yarns. Designed by Nancy Jacobsen for the American Wool Council.

55

Floral Wall Hanging is easy and inexpensive to make using Velverette Craft Glue. Designed by Constance Spates.

For project how-to's, see index on page 89.

47

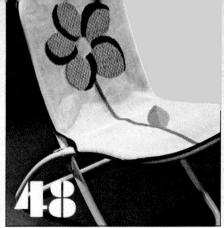

48

49

50-53

54

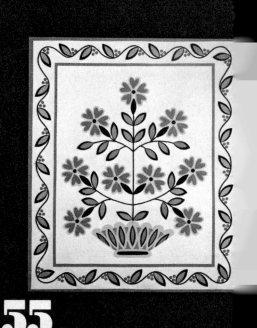

55

56

57

58

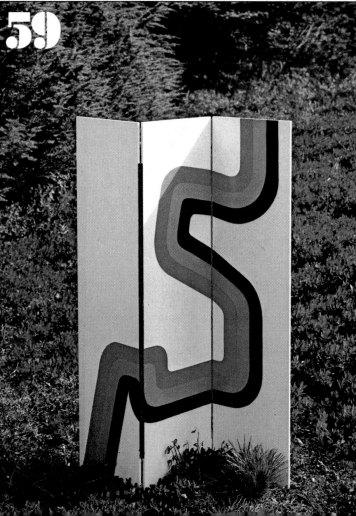

59

INDEX FOR PROJECT DIRECTIONS

56-59

Customized plywood screens make practical additions to any room in the house. In undefined areas, they make great room dividers. Use one to separate living and dining areas. In the bedroom, it separates work area from sleeping area. Placed in a corner, a screen can hide clutter. These screens are easily made from American Plywood panels and then decorated to suit your style. The traditional Pennsylvania Dutch motif is traced onto plywood and then painted with acrylic paints. For a natural look, glue cedar strips on a screen in a diagonal pattern. Mirror-tiled screen expands space in a small room. Graphic design is traced onto plywood and painted in acrylics for a distinctly modern look.

For project how-to's, see index.

(Continued from page 34)

two 16″ wide x 15½″ high ends and two 15″ wide x 15½″ high ends. Nail cubes together with finishing nails. Cut a 17″ square of fabric for cube top (this allows for 1″ overhang).

FABRIC COVERED CUBE

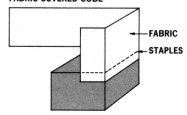

Staple fabric around edges. Cut a length of fabric to cover four sides plus 2″ overhang at top. Staple 1″ edge of fabric to top edge of cube, right side of fabric against cube (see diagram). Pull fabric down, right side out, and staple fabric underneath cube. Place glass on top.

FABRIC COVERED PEDESTAL
MATERIALS: ½″ interior plywood, 1 sheet of 4'x8'; approximately 3 yds. fabric; staple gun; finishing nails.

DIRECTIONS: Cut plywood as follows: 1 piece 10″x10″ (top); 2 pieces 10″x35½″ (sides); 2 pieces 9″x35½″ (sides). Nail pedestal together with finishing nails. Cover with fabric, following directions for FABRIC-COVERED CUBES.

DECORATING WITH SHEETS

Because your decorating needs will be different from ours due to window sizes, table differences and wall expanses, we urge you to take careful measurements. Consult the Fieldcrest chart on this page for sheet sizes, and figure your needs mathematically before you begin. Leftover sheeting from decorating projects is great for throw pillows, napkins, place mats, pillows and cushions. Remember also to watch for white sales for super bargains. **(Note:** For further details and instructions on home decorating projects with sheets, send $1.00 with name and address to: Fieldcrest "Decorating Digest," Fieldcrest, 60 West 40th Street, New York, N.Y. 10018, Att: Publicity Department).

SHEET YARDAGE CHART*
The chart below gives yardage equivalents for two sheet styles: the separate attached hem (often in a contrasting color or pattern), and the self-hem (turned under). The length before hemming is altered slightly, depending on hem type. It is easy and economical to incorporate the hems into projects whenever possible. You may wish to refer to the following chart of sizes *before hemming* when planning your projects.

Flat Sheet Size	Approx. Yardage in fabric		
	36″	45″	58″
Twin	5	4	3 ⅛
Full (Double)	6	4 ¾	3 ⅞
Queen	7	5 ⅞	4 ½
King	8 ¾	7	5 ⅜

Fitted Sheets	Mattress Size
Twin	39″ x 75″
Full (Double)	54″ x 75″
Queen	60″ x 80″
King	72″ x 84″

Attached Hem (Separate)	Self Hem (Turned Under)
66″ x 94″	66″ x 104″
81″ x 94″	81″ x 104″
90″ x 100″	90″ x 110″
108″ x 100″	108″ x 110″

NOTE: If seams are let out on all four corners, this allows an additional 8 or 9 inches on each side.

*Chart and information courtesy of Fieldcrest.

SHEETS FOR ROUND TABLECLOTHS

Cloth Diameter (Add 1″ for hem)	Flat Sheet Required
Up to 65″	Twin
Up to 80″	Full (Double)
Up to 89″	Queen
Up to 99″	King (separate hem)
Up to 107″	King (self hem)

RUFFLED ROUND TABLECLOTH

(page 68-69)

MATERIALS: One double flat sheet, or refer to chart above for fabric equivalent; thread to match; tape measure; sharp scissors; non-stretchy cord; pencil.

DIRECTIONS: Follow directions for making PLAID ROUND TABLECLOTH on page 92.
To make ruffle: Measure circumference of finished tablecloth. Cut a strip 6″ wide and twice as long as circumference, piecing if necessary. Press under ⅛″ and ⅛″ again on both long sides of strip. Stitch close to folded edge. Make 2 rows of long gathered stitches 1½″ from one long edge. Gather to fit and machine stitch to tablecloth with bottom edges even.

PILLOWS AND CUSHIONS

(pages 68-69, 73 and 74)

MATERIALS: One pillowcase or twin flat sheet, depending on size and number to be made; muslin; polyester fiberfill; matching thread.

DIRECTIONS: For each pillow or cushion, cut two square, rectangular or round pieces in desired size from both muslin and sheet fabric. Stitch two muslin pieces together with a ¼″ seam, right sides facing, leaving a 4″ opening for stuffing. Press seams open; turn right side out; stuff with fiberfill; slipstitch opening closed. Stitch two pieces of sheet fabric together with ¼″ seam, right sides facing, leaving opening to insert muslin pillow. (A ruffle can be added if you wish.) Press seams open; turn right side out; slide muslin pillow inside; slipstitch seam closed.

RUFFLED LAMP SHADE

(pages 68-69)

MATERIALS: Twin flat sheet, or see chart on this page for fabric equivalent; ¼″ elastic; ½″ grosgrain ribbon; scissors.

DIRECTIONS: Measure lamp shade top to bottom and distance around. Add 5″ to the height measurement and double the measurement for distance around. Cut fabric to these dimensions. Seam the short ends together. Fold raw top edge under ¼″. Turn the folded edge down 1″. Stitch close to folded edge, leaving an opening to insert elastic. Stitch again ½″ from previous stitching to form casing. Cut elastic and run it through the casing, drawing it up so the cover fits the shade snugly. Cut off excess elastic; sew ends together. Close opening by hand. Fold raw bottom edge up ¼″; turn folded edge up 1½″. Stitch close to folded edge, leaving an opening to insert elastic. Stitch again ½″ from previous stitching to form casing. Again, run elastic through casing and draw up so cover fits shade snugly. Cut off excess elastic; sew ends together. Close opening by hand. Tie ribbon around shade at top and bottom.

FABRIC-COVERED BOX

(pages 68-69)

MATERIALS: Twin flat sheet, or refer to chart on this page for fabric equivalent; wooden box from craft or hobby store; polyester batting; staple gun; white glue; spray adhesive; felt to cover inside of box.

DIRECTIONS: Cover box with pieces of polyester batting, using spray adhesive. Place sheet on a flat surface. Place box on it and cut fabric so that a sufficient amount extends on all sides to cover sides plus about 1″ extra. Place box in exact center of fabric cut to above instructions. Bring fabric up on two opposite sides of box. Fold over rim and staple to inside of box. Fold fabric neatly in at corners and bring up remaining two sides. Fold over rim and staple to inside. Repeat with lid. Cut pieces of felt to fit all inside areas and glue in place.

FABRIC-COVERED LAMP SHADE

(page 73)

MATERIALS: One king size pillowcase, or refer to chart on page 90 for fabric equivalent; paper for pattern; pencil; ruler or tape measure; sharp scissors; spray adhesive; cording for piping; washable white glue; paper clips.

(**Note:** A king size pillowcase is sufficient for one average-size lamp; for more than one lamp, or an extra-large one, you may need to buy a twin flat sheet.)

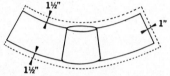

DIRECTIONS—Making Pattern: Lay side of shade on paper; mark top and bottom points of shade (see diagram). Roll shade along paper, marking top and bottom points as you go along. Add 1½" to top and bottom edges of arc for gluing allowance and 1" to one end of arc for overlap. Cut out pattern; place around shade to test for fit and make adjustments, if necessary. **Cutting and Gluing Fabric:** Using pattern, cut out fabric. Spray fabric evenly with adhesive. Carefully press fabric onto shade, smoothing out wrinkles, leaving 1½" allowance at top and bottom edges and overlapping ends; turn under edges and press firmly to inside of shade. **Finishing:** Make piping by cutting a 3"-wide strip of fabric along the bias, 1" longer than circumference of bottom of shade. (If necessary, seam bias strips on the straight grain.) Cut 2 pieces of cording to length of fabric strip. Lay cording pieces along fabric strip, parallel to each other. Fold fabric edges over, overlapping in center, and covering cording; pull taut. Sew through fabric layers along center between cording pieces. Glue finished piping to bottom edge of shade with white glue, trimming excess to match ends. Attach paper clips to help keep piping in place until glue dries.

FABRIC-COVERED PICTURE FRAME

(page 73)

MATERIALS: One twin pillowcase, or refer to chart on page 90 for fabric equivalent; wood stretcher to fit photo or picture to be framed (available at art supply store); paper for pattern; tape measure; ruler; sharp scissors; quilt batting; spray adhesive; masonite, crescent board or stiff cardboard (for back of frame); stiff cardboard (for stand); white or household glue; staple gun or hammer and tacks.

DIRECTIONS—Applying Batting—Front: Trace assembled stretcher dimensions onto paper, carefully drawing around outside and inside edges; cut out pattern. Using pattern, cut out 3 pieces of batting for front. **Sides:** Make pattern, measuring 1" longer than total of outside edges of stretcher x depth of stretcher; cut out 3 pieces of batting for sides. Spraying one side of each piece with adhesive, apply batting to stretcher, covering front and sides layer by layer, allow each layer to dry completely before continuing with next layer; be sure to overlap side ends. **Applying Fabric—Cutting Strips:** Measure height and width of batting-covered frame, adding 4" to each measurement. Then measure girth of frame, wrapping tape measure around one side (see diagram). Cut out two strips of fabric, measuring height x girth, and two strips measuring width x girth. **Covering Frame:** First, cover height sides of frame, one at a time (see diagram).

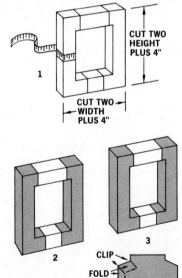

Spray wrong side of fabric piece with adhesive; apply to frame, smoothing down and clipping with scissors to fit neatly. Allow fabric to extend over short end of frame. Repeat with second side. Spray one of the two width pieces with adhesive; clip and fold two ends to make mitered corners (see diagram). Smooth into place, tucking sides under; repeat with second piece of fabric. Let dry completely. **Finishing:** Cut masonite, crescent board or stiff cardboard to make back for frame. Cut rectangle for stand from cardboard; bend back 2". Glue 2" part of stand onto frame back with white or household glue. Let dry completely. Insert picture or photo between frame and back. Staple or tack back onto frame.

(**Note:** You can cover back and stand with fabric before joining, if desired).

SQUARE TABLE SKIRT

(page 73)

MATERIALS: One twin flat sheet, or refer to chart on page 90 for fabric equivalent; pencil; ruler or tape measure; sharp scissors.

DIRECTIONS:—Measuring Fabric—Top: Measure top of table and add ½" to each side; cut fabric for top. **Skirt:** Measure distance around table top and add 6-10 inches for each corner, depending on size of table. (This is the width.) Measure from top of table to floor and add 3" for hem and seam. (This is the length.) Cut fabric for skirt.

Assembling: Starting at one of the short ends of skirt piece, take half of a side measurement, plus ½"; pin to mark. For corner, make a 6"-10" tuck, depending upon original allowance made (see diagram). Pin in place;

stitch ½" down from top. Press in a flat pleat all the way to bottom. Make a second tuck and pleat, one side length from first tuck. Repeat for third and fourth tucks. Fold under ½" at each short end of skirt piece and hem. Pin side to top, matching corners and overlapping ends. Stitch a ½" seam on all four sides, being careful not to catch pleats. Press seam toward sides. Press under ¼" at bottom. Press in a 2¼" hem and blind stitch in place.

FLOWERED PILLOW SHAM

(page 74)

MATERIALS: One twin flat sheet; heavy scissors; ruler; 1 yd. interfacing; 1 package cording; straight pins; thread to match sheet; 20"x26" pillow.

DIRECTIONS: Cut the following from sheet: one 20½"x26½" piece (front of pillow); two 12"x26½" pieces (back of pillow); two 9"x30" pieces (short sides of sham); two 9"x36" pieces (long sides of sham). Cut interfacing into two 4½"x36" pieces and two 4½"x30" pieces. Stitch cording around front piece, using ¼" seam. Hem one lengthwise edge on both back pieces, using ½" seam. Overlap these pieces to measure 20½"; stitch. Place a 9"x36" piece (for long side of sham) and a 9"x30" piece (for short side of sham), right sides together, on work surface. Mark a V, starting 4½"

down one long side to a point 4½" on edge of short side, then to a point 4½" down second long side; stitch; trim excess. Repeat until all pieces for sham are connected, alternating lengths of sham pieces. Trim excess fabric on all joinings. Press seams open; turn right side out; press in half. Stitch interfacing to inside of sham; run a double line of basting stitches along each open side of sham; pull one end of each basted thread until the basted areas have been gathered enough to make the short sides 20½" and the long sides 26". Pin sham to pillow front; stitch with ½" seam; stitch pillow back to pillow front. Press seams open; turn right side out; press. Insert pillow.
(Note: For matching round table-cloth, see directions on this page, for PLAID ROUND TABLECLOTH.)

WINDOW SHADE

(page 74)

MATERIALS: One twin flat sheet, or see chart on page 90 for fabric equivalents; white sheet or cotton drapery lining; roller and slat (from old shade or purchased); 18"-wide fusible webbing (enough to cover shade); masking tape; steam iron; carpenter's square; yardstick; scissors; white glue; shade pull; staple gun (optional).
DIRECTIONS: Cut a section of print sheet and white sheet 1" wider than shade roller, and 12" longer than window opening. Make a small mark at center top and bottom on each piece. Cut strips of fusible webbing and place between the sheets. Overlap webbing as needed so fabric is entirely covered. Smooth layers in place. Following manufacturer's directions, use a steam iron and a wet press cloth to steam press in each position until entire fabric has been bonded. Let fabric cool; turn it over and repeat process on other side. Start in center and work to sides to keep bubbles and wrinkles from being trapped in center.
To finish: Square shade by using a carpenter's square and yardstick. Mark the two long edges first, making sure they are parallel. Then mark and square the short ends. Finished shade width should be slightly shorter than roller. Cut edges smoothly with scissors. Treat edges to prevent raveling by putting a drop of white glue on your finger. Draw you finger slowly along the cut edge, allowing the glue to just barely touch the fabric. A small bead of glue will remain on the shade. Wipe off any excess glue. Turn up 1½" slat hem on bottom of shade. Carefully stitch in place, keeping hem straight and even. Insert slat. Or, fuse a 1" strip of white sheet and fusible

webbing over hem. Attach shade pull. Attach shade to roller along straight line with masking tape. Roll up gently and put in brackets. Or, staple shade to roller, if desired. Adjust shade if needed so it rolls straight.

PLAID WINDOW SEAT COVER

(page 74)

MATERIALS: One twin flat sheet, or refer to chart on page 90 for fabric equivalent; thread to match; tape measure; sharp scissors; one heavy-duty zipper, approximately 6" shorter than length of window seat (or as long as possible); cording for piping, enough for twice the circumference of the cushion.
DIRECTIONS: Cut the sheet to the following dimensions: Measure the length and width of the window seat cushion; add ½" seam allowance around all edges. Cut 2 pieces. Measure the thickness of the cushion at the sides; add ½" seam allowance to each side, then measure the distance around the front and two sides of cushion, add 2"; cut one strip. Measure the length of the long back side of the cushion; subtract 2"; add 3" to the thickness measurement; cut one strip. Cut the back side strip in half lengthwise. Place these strips right sides together and machine baste a ½" seam along one long edge. Stitch over basting 2" into each end. Press open. Center heavy-duty zipper over seam; stitch around all four sides. Remove basting. Join zippered strip to front and side strip with ½" seams on the two short ends. (**Note:** Before stitching, encircle cushion with the pinned strip to make sure it fits snugly.) **To make piping:** Cut two 1" strips on the bias of the fabric to the length of the cording (**Note:** If necessary, seam bias strips on the straight grain.) Fold bias strips in half lengthwise over cording; stitch through both thicknesses close to cording with a zipper foot. With right side up, pin piping to seat cover top on seamline, so that covered cording is to the inside. Stitch all around through all thicknesses. Repeat with seat cover bottom. With right sides together, stitch side strip to top and bottom pieces, making sure that piping allowance is caught in seam and that covered cording is not. Turn right side out, insert cushion, zip closed.

PLAID ROUND TABLECLOTH

(page 74)

MATERIALS: One double flat sheet, or refer to chart on page 90 for fabric equivalent; thread to match; tape measure; straight pins;

sharp scissors; non-stretchy cord or string; pencil.
DIRECTIONS: Measure the diameter of the table, then the distance from table top to floor. For length and width of fabric needed, add diameter of table, plus 2 times the distance from table top to floor, plus 1" for hem. Fold sheet, right sides together, in half, lengthwise, then in half, crosswise, to make a rectangle 4 layers thick. Using non-stretchy cord to serve as a compass, knot one end and pin to center corner of fabric. Tie a pencil to other end of string. Length should be half of diameter of table, plus distance to floor, plus ½". Mark the outer edge of cloth with pencil; cut with sharp scissors. Stitch a ½" finished hem around cloth; press.

PLAID DOUBLE CAFÉ CURTAINS

(page 74)

MATERIALS: One double flat sheet, or refer to chart on page 90 for fabric equivalent; thread to match; tape measure; sharp scissors; drapery weights; café curtain rods in desired width.
DIRECTIONS: (**Note:** You will make four identical pieces and hang them in pairs.) Measure window height and width. Cut 4 rectangles 6" longer than half the window height and the width of the window. Stitch under ¼" on each raw edge. Make a ½" hem on the two sides of each piece. For the top casings, turn under 1" and stitch close to the edge over previous stitching. Press up a 2½" bottom hem; hand-sew drapery weights to hem side; blind stitch hem in place. Hang curtain rods at top and 2" above center of window. Slide one pair of curtains on each rod.

FABRIC-COVERED PARSONS TABLES

Parsons tables come in a variety of sizes and materials. We used 16"-square plastic tables.
MATERIALS: 1 standard-size pillowcase, or see chart on page 90 for fabric equivalents; one 16"-square plastic Parsons table; ruler; white glue; soft brush for glue; sharp scissors; tack cloth; straight pins; thread to match fabric.
DIRECTIONS: Measure a 24½"-square piece from pillowcase for top and side and cut with sharp scissors; measure and cut four 14¾"x10" strips for legs. Center fabric for table top, wrong-side up, over table and pin darts at corner edges; stitch. Slash darts and press open; turn right-side out. Stitch a ½" seam, lengthwise, on strips for legs; press seams open. Pull

right-side out. Slide onto legs; turn raw edges under and glue to top and bottom of legs. Brush white glue over top and sides of table; let dry until a sticky consistency. Pull fabric cover over table top, pressing firmly to adhere fabric to top surface (a paint roller can help smooth fabric on top); overlap raw edge at top of legs. Turn raw edges under and glue to bottom of table, slashing and turning fabric at legs, where necessary. Press fabric on sides of table to adhere securely.

COVERING WALLS WITH FABRIC

(Note: Also see the directions for WASHABLE SHIRRED WALLS, page 37.) This is an excellent way to conceal unwanted colors or textures on walls or to hide walls in poor condition. You can use sheets or fabric bolts in this project, and directions are given for measuring the amount needed for both. Use the staple technique for attaching either to the wall.
MATERIALS: Fabric or sheets to cover walls; yardstick or metal tape measure; chalk, string and set of keys (for plumb line); push pins; sharp scissors; electric or manual staple gun; staples; sharp razor knife; metal-edge ruler.
DIRECTIONS:
Determining the Amount of Fabric Needed When Working with Bolts of Fabric:
Measure the width of each wall in inches with yardstick or metal tape, not a tape measure. Add the widths of the 4 walls to get a total width and divide this by the width of the fabric chosen. If your room is 12'x10', then the walls, in inches, would be 144" + 144" + 120" + 120", for a total of 528". If the width of the fabric is 48", divide 528" by 48" for a total of 11 widths of fabric. (Note: If the total were 11½ widths, then the measurements would have to be made on 12 widths, since any fraction requires that you increase to the next highest number.) Measure the height of the room from ceiling to baseboard and multiply that number by the number of lengths of fabric. For example, if the height of the room from ceiling to baseboard is 95", multiply by 11 widths for a total of 1045". Divide this number by 36" to get the number of yards required. (Our 12'x10' room would be 1045" divided by 36", or 29 yds. of 48" fabric.) Your project will be most economical if you shop around until you find a fabric you like on sale in the quantity you'll need. (White sales offer excellent bargains.)

These measurements do not take into account a pattern that needs to be matched. If this is necessary, measure the number of inches between pattern repeats and add this number to the length of each panel of fabric needed.
Determining the Amount of Fabric Needed When Working with Sheets: Measure the width of each wall in inches and add the 4 measurements. Divide this number by the width of the sheets you have chosen. (See SHEET YARDAGE CHART, page 90.) For example, if your room is 12'x10', it is 144" by 120", and the total is 144" + 144" + 120" + 120", or 528". Now divide this number by the various widths of sheets. It would take 8 sheets if you're working with twin-size, 6½ with double sheets, 6 with queen-size sheets, and 5 with king-size. Since sheets with self-hems are between 104" and 110" long, each sheet will be long enough to cover the average wall height; if your ceilings are extra high, adjustments will have to be made.

These measurements do not take into account patterns that need to be matched. Check the number of inches between pattern repeats and the height of the walls before buying the sheets. If there is a 12" space between pattern repeats and your walls are 95" from the baseboard, only queen- and king-size sheets will be long enough.
Stapling:
(To make staples less conspicuous, you may wish to paint them the background color of the fabric before loading into staple gun.)
1. Cut the fabric or sheets the height of the walls, plus 3".
2. Since few walls are perfectly straight, you'll have to establish a true vertical line that will insure that the fabric hangs straight. To do this, establish a plumb line on first wall by attaching a string to a plumb bob or a set of keys; rub string with chalk. Attach string to a point near the ceiling that is about 1" less than the width of the first fabric panel or sheet. Hold the keys taut at baseboard and snap string. The vertical mark is your guide for hanging first panel.
3. Starting at first corner and using chalk line to keep right side of fabric straight, hang fabric or sheet in place on wall with push pins along top.
4. Staple top in place every 2", leaving excess fabric on ceiling to be trimmed later.
5. Smooth fabric down entire wall, pulling gently, but do not overstretch material. Staple fabric at baseboard, every 2", keeping fabric taut. Staple one side, then the other.
6. Push pin second piece of fabric in place, turning selvage under and overlapping selvage on previous material. Staple in place. Continue until room is covered in fabric, cutting material to fit around windows and doors.
Finishing:
Trim excess fabric from ceiling and

baseboard with a sharp razor blade and a metal-edge ruler. If you did not paint staples to match your fabric, you may wish to cover them with decorative trim or welting.

BORDERED RUG

(pages 70-71)
MATERIALS: 12'x10' piece of carpet; 12'x4' piece of carpet for border (see Note); large scissors or sharp knife; latex adhesive; carpet tape; Scotchgard® Carpet Protector.
DIRECTIONS: This method will create, in the most economical and simplest way, a rug 12 feet wide by 14 feet deep with a one-foot-wide border in a contrasting color. Remember that carpet or broadloom is manufactured in 12-foot widths. First a 12'x10' piece of carpet is ordered for the center, utilizing the carpet's width. For the border, a 12'x4' piece of carpet is needed, again utilizing the carpet's 12-foot width. This piece is then cut into four 12-foot strips that are each one foot wide. Two strips are used to border the 12-foot sides of your 12'x10' carpet; the other two are lined up on the 10-foot sides. Join carpet pieces with latex adhesive and carpet tape, following manufacturer's directions. To prevent edges of carpeting from fraying, cement carpet tape to the backing threads with latex adhesive. When this process is completed, spray entire rug with Scotchgard® Carpet Protector for easy upkeep.
(Note: Carpet with strong directional texture should not be used.)

HAREM PILLOWS

(pages 70-71)
MATERIALS: Fabric for pillow; muslin for liner pillow; zipper (zipper must be at least 5" shorter than one side of pillow in order to tie corners); string; polyester fiberfill.

DIRECTIONS: Cut out two squares or rectangles of fabric (ours are approximately 15" square). Sew a knife edge pillow, right sides facing, inserting a zipper in one side. (Note: Zipper must be at least 5" shorter than the seam so corners can be tied later.) Wrap and tie string securely around each corner about 2" in from the seams. Turn pillow right side out. Sew a liner pillow from muslin, making it an inch or two larger than the outer case. Stuff with fiberfill. Do not tie the corners. The corners of the liner will stuff into the shape of the outer pillow creating the harem pillow's unique shape. Insert liner pillow into fabric cover.

CARPET SQUARE EXERCISE AREA

(page 73)

Carpet squares are simple to install and require a minimum of equipment. The room shown on page 73 was covered with the squares in less than 3 hours. Our room was 12'x17' and worked out perfectly using the total amount of 12" squares packed in one 50-square box and one 10- and three 50-square boxes adhesive-backed vinyl floor tiles. If your room is a different size, start with our design shown here, and see how you can work out a design that ends up using carpet squares and floor tiles in batches of either 50 or 10. To calculate the number of squares needed, simply multiply the length of the room in feet by the width in feet. That number is the number of 12" carpet squares and floor tiles required. If the result is a fraction, go up to the next highest number. When buying the squares and floor tiles, be sure that the lot number and grade letter are the same on all cartons, so that you won't have variations in color or shade.

MATERIALS: One box, fifty 12" self-sticking carpet squares (we used Armstrong's Electoral Brown #450-191); two boxes, fifty 12" squares and one box, ten 12" squares, peel paper and press into place vinyl floor tiles (we used Armstrong's Solarian King Steel #26040); string; chalk; carpenter's right angle or yardstick; soft lead pencil; razor-blade knife or sharp scissors; paper; metal door trim or reducer strips, cut to fit exposed edges in doorways (optional).

DIRECTIONS—Preparing Floor: Be sure floor surface is clean, dry and warm (not below 55°F). Concrete should be vacuumed or washed with warm water and allowed to dry. Remove quarter-round molding from around base of wall; reserve for later reinstallation. Remove furniture and as many other movable objects as possible. Remove any loose, flaking coating from sub-floor and repair any holes or rough spots.

Measuring Floor: Divide the room into quarters: Locate the center points of end (smaller) walls and connect these points by striking a chalk line down middle of the room. Find the center of this chalk line; using a carpenter's angle or yardstick; draw a perpendicular line approximately 2' long on either side of this center. On perpendicular line, strike a second chalk line connecting the two side walls. The room is now divided into quarters. Lay two rows of carpet squares, face down, one from the center of the room to one side wall, the other from the room's center to one end wall; make sure that the edges

of the carpet squares are exactly on the chalk lines. Measure the distance between the last carpet square and the side wall; if it is less than 6" wide, make a new chalk line either 6" closer or farther from the wall. (This prevents you from having to cut too many squares into small border pieces.) Repeat process, if necessary, for end wall and second chalk line. The intersection between the final two chalk lines is the starting point for carpet square and tile installation.

Installing Carpet Squares and Floor Tiles:

1. Place cartons of squares next to work area. Keep all squares with the arrows pointing in the same direction.
2. Begin at the center point. Remove paper from back of first square. Lay square exactly on the two chalk lines, pressing down firmly and making sure that the edges are even with the chalk lines. (**Note:** A few drops of water lightly sprinkled on the self-stick back will help adhesion to floor, but do *not* rub.) Continue placing squares (see diagram for arrangement), making

CARPET SQUARE EXERCISE AREA   1 SQ.=1'

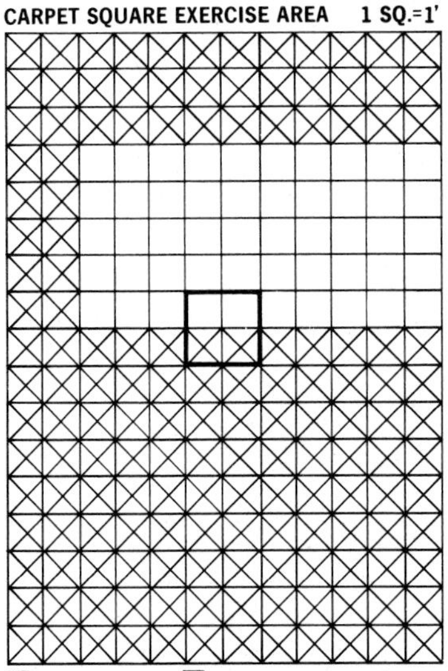

⊠ FLOOR TILES   ☐ CARPET SQUARES

sure that edges butt against adjoining squares or tiles until one quarter of the room is covered with as many whole squares as possible. (Smaller carpet pieces for the border will be cut later, if necessary.) Install vinyl floor tiles, following directions on page 35. Repeat process, a quarter at a time, until all full squares have been installed. (**Note:** If a square gets damaged and must be removed, wet a clean cloth and place over square. Press with a steam iron set on synthetic fabric setting; steam the square until loose. Remove square, noting direction of arrow on back; replace with a new square, making sure that the arrow goes in the same direction. Never iron directly on square, since it may melt.)
3. Cut squares for border area by placing a loose square on top of the

last full square in any row, making sure that the arrows point in the right direction. Place another tile on top of this and slide it until it butts against the wall. Mark the bottom loose square with a soft lead pencil, using top square as a guide. Cut the square along pencil line with a razor-blade knife or sharp scissors (if you use a knife, place a piece of wood under the tile as a cutting surface). Making sure the arrows are still pointing in the right direction, butt the factory edge against the adjoining square and the cut edge against the baseboard; press down firmly. Repeat to cover entire border area.
4. To fit squares around pipes and other irregular shapes, make a paper pattern. (It's best to use a 12" square piece of paper, fitting it into adjoining tiles as you make the pattern.) Check the direction of the arrow and place carpet square on top of pattern. Turn over both carpet square and pattern together; trace pattern onto back of carpet square. Cut square with knife or scissors. Install squares.
5. Replace quarter-round molding around wall edge. Install metal door trim or reducer strips on exposed edges in doorways, if you wish.

FABRIC CANOPY FOR CANOPY BED

(page 76)

MATERIALS: Fabric, cutting and measuring directions follow (**Note:** Fabric should be at least 54" wide); thread to match; small upholstery tacks, hammer; two ¼" gold rings for each tie band; 1" wide twill tape or webbing to measure around top of frame.

Amount of fabric needed—Top: Measure length and width of top of frame and add 1" to each side. (**Note:** If it is necessary to seam the fabric to get the proper width, divide the area lengthwise into thirds and make two ½" seams.) For example, our fabric was 55" wide and our top measured 88" x 65", or 90" x 67" with 1" added to each side. We used two widths of fabric x the length of the top of the frame (90" each), or 5 yards of fabric to make the whole top. **Overhang:** Measure around outside edges at top of frame, going inside the posts. Cut a piece of fabric (seaming as necessary) 18" wide and as long as the outside measurement plus 5" for seams and overlap. Our canopy needed a piece of fabric 238" long, so we used 2¾ yards of fabric, getting three 18" widths and making two seams. (**Note:** Make sure to add ½" to each end for all seams.) **Corner drapes:** Measure length from bottom of the top bar of frame to 1″ above the floor. Add 3½″ to this measurement for seams and hem, and cut sixteen (or eight, if you only want two drapes in two corners) pieces of fabric this length x 27″ wide. We made eight drapes, two in each corner (each drape uses one width of 54″-wide fabric for two 27″-wide pieces.) Therefore, we used 17⅛ yards of fabric for eight drapes, each 77″ high, including extra for hem. The total yardage needed for the canopy was 25 yards, rounding off to allow for tie bands and corner covers. **Tie Bands:** For each band desired (we used four), cut one piece of fabric 14½″ x 6½″. **Inside Corner Covers:** Cut four pieces of fabric, each 22″ x 4½″.

DIRECTIONS—To make top: After making, and pressing seams open, if necessary, turn under ½″ and ½″ again on all edges toward seamed side. Tack top all around to frame, seam side up. **To make overhang:** Piece fabric strip, if necessary, with ½″ seams; press seams open. With right sides together, fold strip in half lengthwise; stitch a ½″ seam along all raw edges, leaving an opening on long edge for turning. Turn; press; whipstitch opening closed. Lay twill tape or webbing on top of piece, with long edge of tape flush with long seamed edge of finished piece; stitch twill tape or webbing to piece, ½″ from edge, through all thicknesses. Placing side of piece with tape facing out, tack through tape only to inside of top of frame; overlapping ends at one corner, behind post on bed. **To make corner drapes:** Place two pieces for drapes with right sides together and stitch 1″ seams on both long sides and ½″ seam on one short side. Turn to right side; press seamed edges flat. On unfinished edge, press under ½″ and 2½″ again for hem. Blind stitch in place; press firmly. Catch 3″ shut at each end along bottom with loose stitches. Using diagram as a guide, pleat top of each drape. Pin pleats in top short end, starting 2½″ in on either end, then making three 5″ deep tucks with 2½″ between each tuck, leaving 2½″ at opposite end. Following pin markings, stitch 4″ down from top edge. Press tucks open to form 2½″ pleats on back of drape. Catch pleats flat with a whipstitch over top edge. (**Note:** The top edge of each drape should measure 10″ across when finished.) Repeat this process for as many drapes as you wish to have (our bed uses eight drapes, with two drapes meeting in each corner.) With pleats facing out, tack drapes from inside through all thicknesses, directly to the canopy frame, centering each tack in one section of drape (4 tacks), so drapes meet at each corner (see photograph on page 76).

Drapes are inside of the overhang. **To make tie bands:** With right sides together, fold each fabric piece for bands in half lengthwise; stitch ½″ seam along long edge. Press band flat, centering seam and pressing open. Stitch ½″ seam along one short end; trim; turn; press. Turn ½″ to inside on other short end; whipstitch closed. Securely hand tack one small gold ring over seam, ½″ in from one end of band. Repeat with other ring at other end of band. Nail a small tack with a head to outer corner of bed post at desired height. Wrap tie band around both drapes at one corner (or use one band for each drape, if you prefer) and loop small gold rings over tack to hold band in place. Repeat for each corner. **To finish:** Take corner cover pieces and fold 1″ under on each edge; press. Blind stitch raw edges in place along both long sides, leaving the 1″ folded under on short edges free. Using diagram as a guide, lift top of one drape out at end away from corner; hand stitch one short end of corner cover piece underneath, with

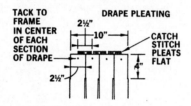

FABRIC CANOPY FOR CANOPY BED

TACK TO FRAME IN CENTER OF EACH SECTION OF DRAPE

DRAPE PLEATING

2½″ 10″ CATCH STITCH PLEATS FLAT

4″

2½″

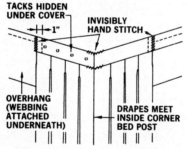

FINISHING WITH CORNER COVERS

TACKS HIDDEN UNDER COVER

1″

INVISIBLY HAND STITCH

OVERHANG (WEBBING ATTACHED UNDERNEATH)

DRAPES MEET INSIDE CORNER BED POST

fold coming over side of drape. Invisibly hand stitch cover piece again to top of inside corner, being careful not to stitch through to front. Lift out opposite end at top of second drape; tuck raw end under, with fold meeting side of drape; invisibly stitch in place.

PATCHWORK PUFF QUILT

(pages 80-81)

MATERIALS (For a 64″x80″ quilt): 10 bags of polyester filling (1 bag will fill eight 8″ squares); solid and print fabrics as desired, cut into 9″ squares (¼ yard of 45″ wide fabric will give you 5 single squares and our quilt used a total of 8 yds.); thread to blend with selected fabrics; sewing needle; scissors.

DIRECTIONS: For each "pillow" square, place two squares of the same fabric with right sides together and stitch a ½″ seam around 3 sides and 1″ into each edge of the fourth side. Turn. Stuff with polyester filling, putting extra fullness in center of pillow; turn ½″ seam allowance in and whipstitch closed. **To make quilt:** Following desired quilt design, place each 2 pillows to be joined with edges even. (**Note:**Make sure all outside edges of quilt are machine-stitched sides of individual "pillows.") Catch edges with small stitches, close together, in an overhand whipstitch, taking in no more fabric than necessary.

SIMPLICITY PILLOWS

(page 82)

CHINTZ PILLOW
MATERIALS: Simplicity pattern #6483; ½ yd. of 35″-36″ or 44″-45″ chintz fabric; ⅝ yd. of 35″-36″ or 44″-45″ chintz fabric for ruffle; ¾ lb. polyester filling.
DIRECTIONS: Follow pattern instructions for View 3 to make this floral chintz pillow, omitting eyelet or lace ruffle.

STRIPED PILLOW
MATERIALS: Simplicity pattern #6483; ½ yd. of 35″-36″ or 44″-45″ striped fabric; ⅝ yd. of 35″-36″ or 44″-45″ plaid fabric for ruffle, ¾ lb. polyester filling.

DIRECTIONS: Follow pattern instructions for View 3 to make this striped pillow with plaid ruffle. Omit eyelet or lace ruffle.

HEART PILLOW
MATERIALS: Simplicity pattern #6483; ½ yd. 35″-36″ or 44″-45″ fabric; 2¾ yds. 2″ flat lace; 2¾ yds. 1½″ flat lace; ¾ lb. polyester stuffing.

DIRECTIONS: With right sides together, stitch short ends of 2″ lace together in ⅜″ seam, forming a circle. Press seam open. Repeat this step with 1½″ lace ruffle. Pin wrong side of 1½″ lace ruffle against right side of 2″ ruffle with raw edges together. To gather, stitch along ⅝″ seam line and ¼″ inside seam line using a long machine stitch. Pin ruffle with 1½″ lace against the right side of one cover. Distribute gathers evenly, allowing extra fullness at the point of the heart. Baste. Follow pattern instructions, using View 4, step 3, to finish.

ALPHABET PILLOWS
MATERIALS: Simplicity pattern #8139; approximately ½ lb. polyester filling for each pillow. You can get 2 of the narrower letters from ½ yd.

of 44" or 45" fabric. Never more than ½ yd. of 35", 36", 44" or 45" fabric, with or without nap, is needed for 1 letter, so it's a good way to use remnants. Suitable fabrics for all pillows are calico prints, broadcloth, chambray, poplin, duck, pinwale corduroy, velveteen or satin (see Buyer's Guide).

DIRECTIONS: Follow pattern instructions for making alphabet pillows. All 26 letters of the alphabet are available.

PENNSYLVANIA DUTCH KNIFE BOX

(page 82)

MATERIALS: ¼" pine for sides and bottom of box (½" wood may be substituted if necessary); ½" pine for box ends and center divider handle; nails; wood glue; medium sandpaper; acrylic paints, green, black, red and white; paint brush; paper for pattern; pencil.

PENNSYLVANIA DUTCH KNIFE BOX

1 SQ.=1"

DIRECTIONS: Follow diagram given for box dimensions. Cut out individual pieces. Glue and nail together. Sand box edges and sides smooth. Pain box green with acrylic paint. While pain dries, enlarge designs to correct size onto paper, following directions on page 37. Transfer designs to box sides and paint appropriate colors. Box can be antiqued with a solution of raw umber oil paint mixed in matte varnish, if you wish. Paint solution over entire box (including designs) and then wipe off with a soft rag.

FABRIC-COVERED PLANTER

(page 82)

MATERIALS: Wooden box; fabric; postcards; ¼" velvet ribbon; vinyl wallpaper paste; ruler; scissors; sharp pencil.

DIRECTIONS: Box may be constructed out of scrap wood or may be bought from an unpainted furniture store. If you make a box, measure the pots first to make sure they will fit inside. Cut a piece of fabric large enough to cover outside of box. Be sure to allow an extra 5" of material at box top and 1" at box bottom to be folded over to inside and to bottom of box. Cover box with vinyl wallpaper paste and adhere fabric to box, one side at a time. Clip fabric at corners and fold to inside and bottom of box. Glue postcards to fabric and frame each in a border of ¼" velvet ribbon. Ribbon is miter cut at edges for a neater appearance.

SPONGE-DECORATED PLANTER CHEST

(page 82)

MATERIALS: ¾" pine boards; nails; wood glue; 2 small hinges; sandpaper; acrylic paint, red oxide and black; paint brush; natural sponge; newspaper; high gloss polyurethane varnish.

SPONGE-DECORATED PLANTER CHEST

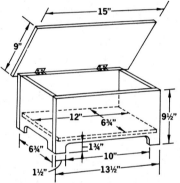

DIRECTIONS: Follow diagram for box size and construction. Cut out individual pieces and glue and nail box together. Attach lid with hinges. Sand box edges and sides smooth. Paint entire box with red oxide acrylic paint. Squeeze black acrylic paint onto a plate and dip sponge into paint. Press sponge lightly onto piece of newspaper to prevent paint from being deposited in solid black onto chest. It will help to practice sponging the paint onto a test board before you apply it to the chest. To finish, give chest a protective coat of high gloss polyurethane varnish after paint is thoroughly dry.

SHAKER CANDLESTICK HOLDER

(page 82)

MATERIALS: ½" pine lumber or other wood; coping saw or jig saw; drill; sandpaper; wood glue; 2 wood screws; 1 wooden peg (see **Note**); wood stain; paper for pattern; pencil.

SHAKER CANDLESTICK HOLDER

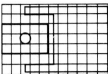

1 SQ.=1"

DIRECTIONS: Following directions on page 37, enlarge and transfer design onto wood. Cut out pieces with a coping saw or jig saw. Sand edges and surfaces smooth. Drill hole in wood for inserting peg. Connect back piece to base with wood glue and two wood screws. Stain with wood stain of your choice.
(**Note:** Shaker pegs available from Woodcraft Supply Corp., 313 Montvale Avenue, Woburn, Mass. 01801. Ten pegs are $2.15.)

RUFFLED FABRIC MIRROR

(page 83)

MATERIALS: Round mirror, 13" diameter; ¾ yd. print fabric; ½ yd. solid color fabric; 2 yds. ½"-wide grosgrain ribbon (choose ribbon and fabrics in colors that complement each other); Wilhold Heavy Body Craft Glue or other white glue paste; scissors; straight pins.

DIRECTIONS: Our mirror frame's puffy pleating is all done with glue. For best results, practice with a 6" strip of fabric (approximately 3" wide) and a 3" square of cardboard. Spread glue along the long edge of fabric, on wrong side. Overlap edge of fabric onto one edge of the cardboard and slide fabric into uneven gathers. Spread glue on other long edge of fabric, on wrong side. Fold fabric around and overlap onto bottom side of cardboard to form a sandwich with cardboard in the middle. Slide fabric into gathers. Spaces between gathers needn't be precise and gathers on front and back shouldn't match up— the differences add to the puffiness. To begin, cut two strips of print fabric 12" wide; cut two strips solid color fabric 7" wide. Fold each strip in half to find the center; mark the center point of each strip with a straight pin. Divide the mirror into four equal sections, marking on front and back. Starting on back of mirror, spread glue on wrong side of one long edge of print fabric and gather and glue all fabric up to pin marker onto one-quarter of mirror edge; gather and glue remaining half of fabric onto second quarter of mirror. Working with second print fabric strip, repeat for other half of mirror, overlapping fabric strips ½". Turn mirror over, spread glue along wrong side of other long edge of fabric and gather and glue to edge of mirror face. Remove straight pins. Allow glue to dry thoroughly (at least 1 hour). To add solid color ruffle, spread glue on right side of one long edge and gather and glue fabric to mirror face, seeing that fabric extends no more than ⅜" onto mirror. Again, one strip of fabric will gather onto half the mirror. Allow glue to dry thoroughly. Then apply glue to wrong side of other long edge. Fold fabric over and gather and glue on top of previously glued edge. Allow glue to dry thoroughly. Apply glue to one side of grosgrain ribbon and glue ribbon carefully over raw edges of fabric on front and back of mirror.

(**Note:** This technique can be used on any size mirror. Simply increase or decrease your fabric and ribbon amounts to accommodate whatever size mirror you have.)

LACY TABLE SETTING

(page 83)

LACY PLACE MATS

MATERIALS: Simplicity pattern #8364; see pattern for fabric requirements; same yardage of lace fabric as for place mat, thread to match; scissors.

DIRECTIONS: Cut lace same as place mat pattern tissue. Sew lace to place mat with right sides together, sewing all corner points and leaving 4" edge open. Trim all seams to ¼". Turn; press. Slipstitch opening closed. (Try to purchase a lace pattern done in an alternating motif stripe. This will enable you to cut floral motif for napkins.)

LACY NAPKINS

MATERIALS: Simplicity pattern #8364; 1 yd. fabric for 4 napkins; lace for edging; thread to match; scissors.

DIRECTIONS: Cut napkin size according to pattern. Turn under seam allowance and clean finish. Cut lace edging to napkin size, being sure to leave enough to fold and stitch at corners.

NAPKIN RINGS

MATERIALS: 7" length of lace for each napkin ring (use leftover scraps from place mats); thread to match; scissors.

DIRECTIONS: With right sides together, stitch short ends of lace together, using ½" seams. Press seams flat. Turn right side out.

STENCIL DESIGN BASKET

(page 83)

The lacy design on our wastebasket is quick and easy to do with spray paint and an unusual "stencil"—a doily. Our instructions include a giant doily to crochet in about half an hour. If you don't crochet, experiment with pieces of flea market lace or crochet. Look for a pattern with large areas of open work and a well-defined design. The spray paint won't wash out, so don't stencil with something you'll want to use again. Before stenciling the basket, make a test of the pattern by laying the stencil flat on a piece of paper and spraying over it. Look at the painted paper from 3 or 4 feet back to see if it "reads."

MATERIALS: Reed wastebasket, approximately 11" high and 12" in diameter at the top; Krylon's Interior/Exterior Spray Enamel, Flat White #1502 and Aqua-Turquoise #2008; 1 skein craft and rug yarn, any color; size K crochet hook; straight pins; newspaper; pencil.

DIRECTIONS: Spray paint the basket inside and out with Flat White, applying 2 or 3 coats for even coverage. Protect the area you are working on with newspaper. Allow basket to dry at least 20 minutes between coats. **Making Crochet Stencil:** With K hook and 2 strands of rug yarn held together, ch 12; sl st to beg ch to form ring. **Rnd 1:** Ch 14, tr in ring; (ch 9, tr in ring) 5 times; ch 9, sl st to 4th ch from bottom of beg ch-14. **Rnd 2:** Ch 8, *sc in middle st of ch-9 loop, ch 4, tr in tr, ch 4. Rpt from * around; end ch 4, sl st in 4th ch of beg ch-8. **Rnd 3:** Ch 4, tr in same sp as sl st (first corner made); *ch 4, tr in sc, ch 4, tr in tr, ch 4, tr in sc, ch 4, 2 tr in tr (corner made). Rpt from * 2 times. For short bottom edge, ch 4, tr in sc, ch 4, sl st to top of beg ch-4. **Rnd 4:** Ch 5, sc in first tr; *work 4 sc in each of next 4 ch-4 loops; sc in first corner tr, ch 5, sc in 2nd corner tr. Rpt from * 2 times; on short side, work 4 sc in each of next 2 ch-4 loops, sl st in base of beg ch-5. Cut yarn, tie and weave in ends. **Stenciling:** Divide basket into 3 equal sections at top edge, marking divisions lightly in pencil. Center doily, narrow side at bottom, on one-third of basket. Doily should be stretched but shouldn't fill whole one-third of basket. Push straight pins through basket weave to hold doily in place, lining up stitches around centered ring at beginning of doily. Pin newspaper to mask inside of basket and other two-thirds of outside. Spray around edges and in all open areas of stencil with Aqua-Turquoise, holding can about 12" from basket. Remove doily im-

mediately and let basket dry thoroughly before repeating stenciling process on other two-thirds of basket.

FLOWER STENCIL BASKET

(page 83)

MATERIALS: Bowl-shaped basket with foot and rim, approximately 10" in diameter and 5½" high; strip of fabric large enough to wrap around basket for stencil; Elmer's Glue-All®; Krylon's Interior/Exterior Spray Enamel, Antique White #1503, Jungle Green #2011, Burnt Orange #2406; paper for pattern; pencil; ruler; scissors; straight pins; masking tape; newspapers.

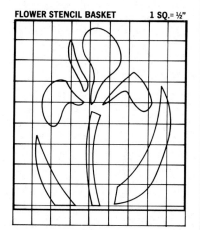

FLOWER STENCIL BASKET   **1 SQ.= ½"**

DIRECTIONS: Cut a strip of fabric long enough to wrap around basket and overlap ½"; it should be 2" wider than the height of basket. Mix a solution of 1 part Elmer's Glue-All and 2 parts water; saturate fabric with glue solution and hang up to dry and stiffen. If basket is made of cane (shiny, nonporous surface), rough up surface with sandpaper. Place basket on a pedestal (such as a coffee can) at a good working height. Protect work surface with newspapers. Spray basket inside and out with Antique White, applying 2 or 3 coats for even color. Allow basket to dry at least 20 minutes between coats. **Cutting the stencil:** You will make one fabric stencil large enough to wrap around basket; it is cut in two stages for the two colors. The stiffened fabric makes a clear, sharp stencil that can be folded to fit the curve at the bottom of the basket. Following directions on page 37, enlarge design on paper. Cut pattern out along border; cut out petal, leaf and stem areas. On stiffened fabric, draw guidelines 1" from top and bottom, and ¼" from each end. Line up paper pattern on bottom guideline at one end of fabric, ¼" in from end. Draw around paper pattern on border, then draw flower on fabric. Repeat at other end of fabric strip. Mark center of fabric strip and center of pattern. Align marks and trace pattern in center of strip. In remaining space, position pattern so spaces between flowers are equal, and trace pattern (we used seven motifs around our basket). Cut out only the flower petals from fabric stencil. **To stencil:** Pin fabric stencil to basket, pushing straight pins through holes in basket weave. Top edge of flower should line up just below rim of basket. Lap top edge of fabric over basket rim. Pin around cut-out areas so stencil lays flat against surface. Place basket on pedestal and spray petals Burnt Orange, keeping spray can about 12″ from surface and using a sweeping motion. Remove stencil immediately, before paint dries. When stencil is dry, cut out stems and leaves. Lining up petals, pin stencil to basket just below rim. Line stems up under each flower and pin flat to bottom of basket and around leaves and stems. Fold top edge of fabric down to expose basket rim for painting. Tape over petal sections of stencil, being careful that tape does not stick to painted basket. Pin a piece of newspaper to inside of basket below rim to mask interior. Place basket on pedestal and spray both rim and leaf stencils with Jungle Green. Remove stencil immediately and allow basket to dry thoroughly. Turn basket upside down; pin newspaper to basket, exposing only foot and bottom of basket. Spray Jungle Green. Allow to dry thoroughly.

SPRAYED BASKET TRAY

(page 83)

MATERIALS: Basket tray, approximately 15″ long, 11″ wide and 2″ deep; 18″ x 15″ fabric strip for stencil; pencils; white glue (we used Elmer's) to stiffen stencil; spray paint (we used Krylon Interior/Exterior Spray Enamel in Antique White #1503, Aqua-Turquoise #2008 and Burnt Orange #2406); sharp scissors; straight pins; aluminum foil or wax paper.

GENERAL DIRECTIONS: An overspray technique was used to soften the edges of the color on this design. Practice it before you begin by laying one piece of paper (stencil) on top of another piece; aim the spray can for the edge of the stencil, letting a spray of paint hit the bottom paper. When the stencil is removed, one edge of color will be sharp, the other fuzzy. Only one stencil cut is made for the tray; the stencil is moved out from this cut to make turquoise spray line and in from cut for orange and white spray lines.

Preparing Fabric: Make a creamy paste of ⅓ glue, ⅔ water; dunk fabric in paste and squeeze out excess. Spread fabric flat on aluminum foil

or wax paper, and let dry completely before cutting.

Preparing Basket: Spray inside and outside of tray with Antique White, using at least 2 coats to get an even color; let dry thoroughly between coats.

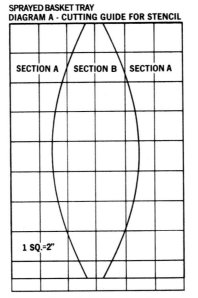

SPRAYED BASKET TRAY
DIAGRAM A - CUTTING GUIDE FOR STENCIL

SECTION A | SECTION B | SECTION A

1 SQ.=2″

Cutting Stencil: Following directions on page 37 enlarge and transfer pattern in Diagram A to fabric and cut out with scissors.

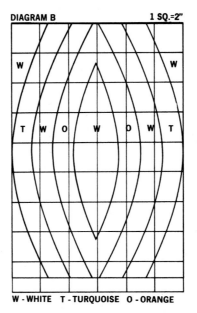

DIAGRAM B   1 SQ.=2″

W — WHITE   T - TURQUOISE   O - ORANGE

To Stencil: Following Diagram B, pin stencils to basket (placing pins between weave) at outer edges of turquoise stripes, gently pressing against sides to fit. Spray with Aqua-Turquoise, just at edge of stencils, allowing color to spread onto white for only an inch or so. Remove stencils immediately and let dry thoroughly. Move stencils in to outer edge of orange stripes; pin in place and spray as for aqua. Remove stencils, let dry, then repeat for central white motif (optional). If desired, turn basket over

and repeat stenciling process on bottom of basket, aligning colors at lip of tray.

TUTTI FRUTTI BOWL

(page 83)

MATERIALS: 2½ qt. translucent white glass mixing bowl; 1 felt square in each of the following colors: emerald green, medium green, light green, dark yellow, yellow, orange, gold, red, hot pink, dark brown, medium brown, rust; scissors; paper for pattern; pencil; newspapers; Scotch Sprament® Adhesive; Scotchgard® fabric protector.

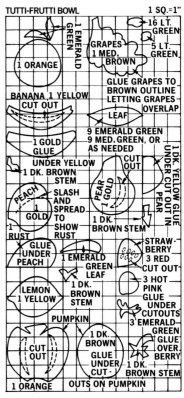

TUTTI-FRUTTI BOWL   1 SQ.=1″

DIRECTIONS: Place bowl on paper and trace base of bowl onto paper. Draw another circle 1″ wider than the first and cut out pattern on this outer circle. Using pattern, cut base circle from emerald green felt. Following directions on page 37, enlarge and cut out fruit and leaf patterns from appropriate colors of felt. Protect work surface with newspapers. Spray all felt pieces with Scotchgard® fabric protector and allow to dry thoroughly. When dry, assemble individual fruits, using spray glue. Spray green felt base circle with glue; place bowl in center and fold felt up around base of bowl, keeping a straight edge. Glue leaf border to rim of bowl, folding each leaf over rim and alternating emerald green and medium green. Allow leaves to overlap slightly, maintaining a straight edge on outside of bowl. Lightly trace outlines of fruit on bowl, starting with pumpkin and working from right to left: pumpkin, peach overlapping pumpkin, orange, lemon overlapping orange, pear overlapping lemon, grapes overlapping pear, strawberries overlapping grapes, banana overlapping pumpkin. Adjust spacing of fruit so they form a complete circle. Spray fruit with glue and adhere to bowl. Allow to dry thoroughly. Avoid washing outside of bowl.

ABSTRACT YARN CANISTER

(page 83)

MATERIALS: 1-pound coffee can; pale aqua spray paint; sport-weight yarn, 1 oz. each in the following colors: rust, orange, navy, green, yellow, beige, turquoise; scissors; pencil; tracing paper; Scotch Spra-Ment Adhesive®; Scotchgard® fabric protector; newspapers.

DIRECTIONS: An interesting patchwork of texture and color can be built up on the outside of a can with glue and yarn, especially if the yarn is applied in a variety of directions. Develop your own pattern or follow our diagram for colors and shapes. It is easiest to work on one-quarter of the can at a time. Spray on Spra-Ment® adhesive rather heavily; lay down yarn colors that define major shapes first, then fill in with the other colors. Lay yarn down from outer edges of a shape to the center, using one continuous strand that is cut when the shape is filled. Work quickly and don't pull yarn taut. **Preparing the can:** Clean can and remove price stamp, if possible. Spray inside and out with paint to cover labeling. Protect work surface with newspapers. Allow can to dry thoroughly. **Making the pattern:** Following directions on page 119, enlarge pattern onto tracing paper. Trace major outlines onto can with pencil. **Applying the yarn:** Spray one-quarter of can with Spra-Ment® adhesive and lay down yarn, following directions above. Protect work surface with newspapers. When glue has dried too much to grab, or section is finished, mask finished work with newspaper, spray next section with

glue and continue filling can's surface with yarn. When finished, spray entire yarn surface with Scotchgard® fabric protector.

ART DECO MIRROR

(page 83)

MATERIALS: 12"x16" lightweight mirror (actual size of most framed mirrors is 14"x18"); 14-ply mat board in the following colors and sizes: 18"x24" pink, 14"x18" brown, 14"x18" light blue; single edge razor blades; straight edge; ruler; pencil; Wilhold Decorator's Craft Glue; clear fixative; adhesive picture/mirror hangers; newspapers.

DIRECTIONS: Measure and cut mat board carefully to ensure straight, clean edges. Work on several layers of newspaper to avoid cutting into work surface. Layers of color on the frame are separated by an extra thickness of mat board cut slightly smaller than the layer above it. Cut these underlay pieces first, as they needn't be as accurate. To cut mat board, measure off all pieces to be cut on a board and draw cutting lines lightly with pencil. With straight edge held firmly on cutting line, draw sharp single edge razor blade along straight edge, exerting pressure. Repeat razor cut several times until mat board is cut through. To begin, cut mat board strips in the following colors and sizes: From pink, cut one 15½"x19½" rectangle, 2 strips 14½"x¾", 2 strips 10½"x¾", four 1¼" squares; from brown, cut 2 strips 15½"x1¾", 2 strips 11½"x1¾", four ¾" squares; from blue, cut 2 strips 15"x1¼", 2 strips 11"x1¼", four 1¾" squares. To cut the underlay, use leftover brown or blue board and mark "underlay" on face of strips to avoid confusion during assembly. Cut 4 strips 1½"x14", 4 strips 1½"x15½", 2 strips 1"x14½", 2 strips 1"x10½", 2 strips ½"x14", 2 strips ½"x10", four 1" squares, four ½" squares.

Assembling mirror: Before gluing, stack parts up to check placement and size. Remove mirror from frame (if it has one) and place mirror on pink rectangle. Arrange 1½" underlay

strips around mirror, using 2 layers, if needed, to reach level of mirror. Arrange blue squares and brown strips on top of underlay and mirror to form frame. Place 1" underlay strips and squares in center of each panel and corner. Place blue strips and pink squares, then ½" underlays. (Pink squares are positioned at right angles to blue squares.) End with pink strips and brown squares.

Gluing the parts: Glue underlay strips to backs of pink and blue panels and brown and pink squares. Glue blue panels to brown panels and pink panels to blue, centering each. Glue pink squares to blue squares, and brown squares to pink. Glue layers of outer underlay together. Remove mirror from pink rectangle. Spray all mat board surfaces with fixative.

To finish: Glue mirror to pink rectangle, centering it. Glue underlay pieces to pink rectangle. Glue panels and corners to underlay and mirror. Attach adhesive hangers to back of mirror.

UPHOLSTERED PICTURE FRAME

(page 83)

MATERIALS: One sheet of 14-ply mat board, 18"x24"; ½ yd. floral print fabric; ½ yd. miniprint fabric to complement floral; ruler; straight edge; single edge razor blades; scissors; small amount polyester fiberfill or quilt batting; Wilhold Body Craft Glue.

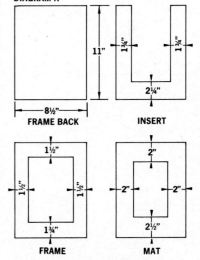

UPHOLSTERED PICTURE FRAMES
DIAGRAM A

DIRECTIONS—Making the frame: With razor blade and straight edge, cut 4 rectangles, 11"x8½", from mat board. Following diagram A for measurements, cut away center sections of 3 rectangles. From floral print fabric, cut two 12"x13½" rectangles and one 8"x10½" rectangle. From miniprint fabric, cut one 12"x13½" rectangle. Place matboard frame sec-

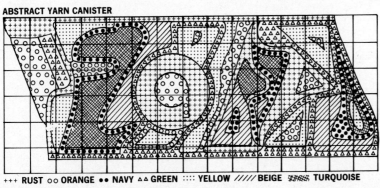

ABSTRACT YARN CANISTER

+++ **RUST** ∘∘ **ORANGE** •• **NAVY** △△ **GREEN** ⠿ **YELLOW** ////// **BEIGE** ⧓⧓⧓ **TURQUOISE**

tion on center of one large floral rectangle and mark and slash fabric at center, as shown in diagram B.

DIAGRAM B

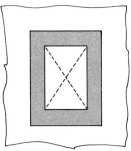

SLASH FABRIC ALONG DOTTED LINE, TO CORNERS OF FRAME

Place matboard mat section on miniprint rectangle and repeat. You will make 2 "sandwiches," for the front and the back of the frame. These will later be glued together, except at the top edge, where the picture slips in. **Assembling back section:** Spread glue on mat board frame back, then add fiberfill, distributing puffiness evenly. Spread out uncut 12″x13½″ floral rectangle, wrong side up. Lay frame back, fiberfill side down, in center of rectangle. Place mat board insert section, cut edge at top of frame, over frame section and glue in place. Spread glue along outer edges of fabric, fold over frame insert and glue in place, mitering corners and pulling fabric taut over fiberfill. Slash fabric at top edge, if needed, to get smooth line around edges of insert. Trim excess fabric. Spread glue along edges of smaller floral rectangle, on wrong side of fabric; glue rectangle to front of back section.
Assembling front section: Center mat board mat section on miniprint fabric, wrong side up. Pull triangles of fabric at center through cut-out in mat and glue to mat board. Fold outer edges of fabric over mat board, pulling fabric taut and mitering corners; glue in place. Spread glue on front of frame section and add a layer of fiberfill, distributing puffiness evenly. Place frame section, fiberfill down, on remaining floral rectangle, wrong side up. Pull fabric triangles to back and glue to mat board. Now, place completed mat section on top of frame section, right side down and outer edges lined up—check that wider borders on bottom edges of frame and mat line up. Fold outer edges of frame fabric over frame and mat sections, pulling fabric taut and mitering corners; glue in place.
Assembling frame: Place frame front and back sections together, fiberfill sides out and bottom edges aligned (cut-out on insert goes on top). Glue together along sides and bottom; add weights until glue dries thoroughly. Slip photo through opening at top.

FABRIC PUFF BASKETS

(page 83)

MATERIALS: 2 baskets with lids, approximately 5½″x3½″ and 7½″x5½″; 1 yd. boldly printed fabric; polyester quilt batting to cover baskets; Scotch Spra-Ment®; Scotch Super Strength Adhesive®; Scotchgard® fabric protector; scissors; 1 yd. ½″-wide grosgrain ribbon.
DIRECTIONS: Since baskets are handmade, they vary in size and in construction details; these directions tell how to measure fabric right from your own baskets. On the baskets we used, the lid fits over a separate flange attached to the inside top edge of the basket. After the basket was finished, we removed the flange (it was stapled) and glued it to the inside edge of the lid to maintain a good fit. Examine your baskets before you start to see how the lid fits and how it can be changed to ensure a good fit after application of the batting and fabric.
Preparing the basket: Cut circles of polyester quilt batting the size of the base and the top of the lid; cut a strip the height of the basket and wide enough to go around it. Spray batting surfaces with Spra-Ment® and pat onto basket. **Cutting the fabric:** Choose the part of the pattern you want to show and cut a strip of fabric 1″ longer than the height of the basket and long enough to wrap around the overlap 1″. Place basket on another section of fabric (wrong side up) and trace a circle the size of the basket base. Draw another circle 2″ out from this one and cut fabric on this outer line. Place lid on fabric (wrong side up) and repeat. **Assembling the basket:** Apply Spra-Ment® to wrong side of fabric circle for bottom of basket. Place basket in center of fabric and fold edges up around basket, easing fabric into pleats as you go. You may need to use the Super Strength Adhesive® to keep pleats in place. For side of basket, spray edges of wrong side of fabric strip with Spra-Ment® and fold a ½″ hem under on all four edges. Spray wrong side of fabric with Spra-Ment® and glue to side of basket —bottom edge will be glued to fabric turned up from base; top edge does not fold over lip of basket. All batting and raw fabric edges should be covered. Spray wrong side of fabric for lid with Spra-Ment®; place lid in center of circle and wrap fabric up over edge of lid, easing fabric into pleats. Again, secure fabric pleats with Super Strength Adhesive®, if needed. Trim fabric on inside of basket lid. Spread Super Strength Adhesive® on grosgrain ribbon and glue over raw fabric edges on inside of lid. Adjust lid to fit basket. Spray fabric with Scotchgard®, following manufacturer's di-

rections.

LACY TABLECLOTH

(page 83)

MATERIALS: Simplicity pattern #8364; see pattern for fabric requirements; lace fabric (see Directions below).
DIRECTIONS: To make lace top tablecloth, be sure to purchase an even-patterned lace that is 60″ in width. Using tissue from pattern, cut around lace motifs to create a finished edge. Follow pattern instructions for making underskirt.

LACY CURTAINS

(page 83)

MATERIALS: Simplicity pattern #5494; 2⅜ yds. of 48″-50″ lace fabric for 36″ length curtains

DIRECTIONS: These curtains will fit windows up to 40″ wide. Using an open lacy fabric with scalloped border edge eliminates the need for hemming. Following pattern instructions for View 3, cut the curtains with the supplied tissue pattern, placing the border at the marked hem edge. Also use bordered edge for the valance ruffle. Follow pattern instructions to complete.

LACE TRIM PILLOW

(page 83)

MATERIALS: Simplicity pattern #6483; ½ yd. of 35″-36″ or 44″-45″ fabric; piece of open lace

DIRECTIONS: Follow pattern instructions for View 3, but before joining the 2 cover sides, topstitch a piece of open lace onto the center. Try to purchase lace that has a uniform design so that the pillow will have a finished look. Complete pillow, following pattern instructions.

ROUND LACE PILLOW

(page 83)

MATERIALS: Simplicity pattern #8138; ½ yd. of 35"-36" or 44"-45" fabric; 1½ yds. pre-gathered crochet-type edging, ½" wide; lace fabric with 4" circle designs.
DIRECTIONS: Cut out pattern pieces following View 1. Cut circle motif out of lace fabric and stitch in center of one pillow cover. Place first row of lace ruffle around circle motif and stitch. Place second row of lace ruffle approximately 1″ from edge of cover and stitch. To finish pillow, follow pattern instructions for View 1.

FAB. U. PRINT® LANCASTER ROSE QUILT

(page 84)

MATERIALS (for 1 queen size quilt; additional fabric is required for making king size quilt and pillows:) 10 yds. 44″-45″ wide fabric, antique white for squares and drop; 6½ yds. 44″-45″ wide fabric, apple green for lattice, crosspieces and borders; 16½ yds. fabric for interlining; 16½ yds. fabric for backing; batting; antique white thread; transparent thread; Fab.U.Print® design paper, in desired colors; iron. (**Note:** Fabric to be printed must be a minimum of 35% polyester for colorfastness; pre-wash all fabric.)

LANCASTER ROSE PATTERN 1 SQ.=½″

ONE-QUARTER SECTION

DIRECTIONS: Following directions on page 37, enlarge pattern pieces and cut 4 of each from the appropriate Fab.U.Print design color. Outside points of hearts are based on 10″ square. Cut 20 pieces of white fabric 14″ square (fabric will shrink slightly during printing and should therefore be cut to finished size after printing). Lay fabric over template of complete pattern; position lattice outline of flower, color side down, on fabric and cover with protective ironing paper. Apply heat 20-30 seconds, moving iron slowly and constantly, and pressing iron firmly. Check density of color and apply more heat if necessary. Position solid color areas inside lattice flower and print as before. Position 4 points and print, followed by 4 hearts, using the template as a guide. Colored pieces may be re-used, adding more time for maintaining color strength. Design paper may also be re-charged. To do so, place design, color side up, on protective ironing paper. Place new sheet of same color design paper, color side down, on top and iron 20-30 seconds. Color will be transferred to the original. Individual

printed squares may be quilted. Use transparent thread to avoid having to change thread colors.

LANCASTER ROSE QUILT

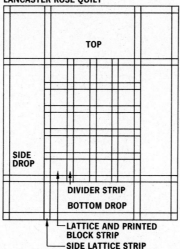

To assemble: Cut printed and quilted blocks to size, allowing for seam allowance. Leave ½″ seam allowance. *Designed blocks:* 20 printed squares, 11″x11″. *Green strips:* 49 lengths, 4″x11″; 30 squares, 4″x4″; 6 lengths, 4″x21″; 2 lengths, 4″x30″. *White border insets:* 1 top, 50″x30″; 1 foot, 50″x21″; 2 sides, 63″x21″; 2 top corners, 21″x31″; 2 bottom corners, 21″x21″. All individual pieces are finished with batting and interlining before joining. Accuracy is extremely important as variation of 1/16″ per piece using this number of pieces is enough to throw off the alignment of the quilt. Lay fabric with piece sizes drawn out in pencil over the batting and interlining and pin together. Use zig-zag stitch and sew on each side of line, then cut pieces apart on lines. To make a guide for joining squares, etc., place a strip of tape on your machine ½″ from needle. Join first row of printed squares by sewing lattice strip to the top of one completed block. Then join the bottom of the block to another lattice strip. Continue this procedure until you have joined 5 quilted blocks with lattice strips on top and bottom of all pieces. Make 4 of these lengths (½″ seams). Join the divider strips in similar fashion; starting with a 4″ square and lattice strip and so on. Make 3 of these lengths. Join completed block and divider strips. After quilted block section is completed, join top and foot pieces. Now assemble 2 side lattice strips (less end square which becomes part of the border). Join these strips to outside edge of completed block section. Make 2 side drop sections— top corner, lattice, side piece, lattice and bottom border. Attach completed side drop sections in similar manner.
Border: All pieces are cut allowing for seams and hem on all sides of finished

spread—2 lengths, 30″x8½″; 2 lengths, 64″x8½″; 6 lengths, 21″x8½″; 2 lengths, 50″x8½″; 8 lengths, 4″x8½″; 4 corners, 8½″x8½″. Press seams toward green strips. Press all seams of small green squares towards their centers. Backing is attached after the outer hem is made.
For double size quilt: Cut green strips 3″ wide instead of 4″. Lengths remain the same.
For king size quilt: Use 4″ green strips as for queen size and add one panel of design blocks in length and two panels in width—36 blocks in total. (Outer lengths will vary.)
For pillows: Join a printed quilted square with lattice strip at top and bottom. Join two side pieces with 4″ squares on each end of lattice strip. Join each of these to the main body of pillow face. Cut pillow back the same size as top section and join, using ½″ seam allowance on all sides. Zipper opening is optional.

SPRAY-PAINTED CHAIRS

(page 84)

MATERIALS: Wood slat chairs; ruler; pencil; tracing paper; masking tape; newspaper; aluminum tape in ¼″, 1″, 1¼″ and 2″ widths; Krylon Spray Paint in the following colors: Glossy White; Dove Grey; Moss Green; Jungle Green; Baby Blue; Purple.

SPRAY-PAINTED CHAIRS

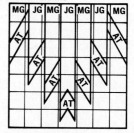

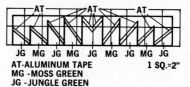

AT-ALUMINUM TAPE   1 SQ.=2″
MG -MOSS GREEN
JG -JUNGLE GREEN

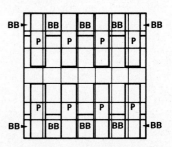

BB - BABY BLUE   P – PURPLE   1 SQ.=2″

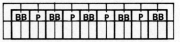

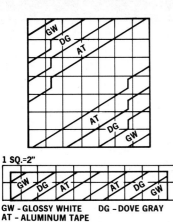

1 SQ.=2"

GW - GLOSSY WHITE   DG - DOVE GRAY
AT - ALUMINUM TAPE

DIRECTIONS: Following directions on page 37, enlarge patterns onto tracing paper. Transfer pattern to chair back and seat, marking lightly with pencil. With masking tape, mark off one color section of the pattern at a time and spray-paint. Allow paint to dry at least 20 minutes before removing tape. Re-tape chair for next color application. After both colors have been applied, remove masking tape and allow second color to dry for at least 20 minutes. Edge design with aluminum tape where indicated. (**Note:** Protect all work surfaces with newspaper.)

REDECORATE A CHAIR

(page 84)

A chair you may have given up on can gain a new identity with the imaginative use of paint and some pretty new seat cushions. We used Fuller O'Brien paints in Orange Flip, Sun Yellow and Wedgwood Blue to spruce up this chair, but any colors that coordinate with your room's decor will do the trick. The seat cushions are a snap (see directions on page 90 for making PILLOWS AND CUSHIONS). We used a Duo-Fast staple gun to attach the dust ruffle around the chair seat and added simple ties to the back cushion for attaching it to the chair. Why not coordinate the cushions with your tablecloth and napkins for a dining room chair, or use colorful sheets for a coodinated bedroom look.

ELEPHANT WALK CHEST

(page 84)

MATERIALS: 1 Hunt/Speedball Fabric Screen Printing Kit (or: 10"x14" screen, stiff piece of cardboard, squeegee, 4 oz. Hunt/Speedball photo emulsion, 1 oz. Hunt/Speedball sensitizer, 4 oz. Hunt/Speedball screen filler, tracing paper, small artist's paint brush); 4 oz. Hunt/Speedball blue textile ink; 4 oz. Hunt/Speedball orange textile ink;

black felt-tipped or India ink pen; cellophane tape; #1 photo flood light bulb; lamp cord with standard socket; disposable cup; sheet of black paper; 10"-12" aluminum pie plate; soft lead pencil; 4-drawer chest from Sears, #1H 12864C.

ELEPHANT WALK CHEST   1 SQ.=1"

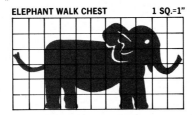

DIRECTIONS: Following directions on page 37, enlarge elephant design onto tracing paper. Fill in the areas to be printed with a black felt-tipped pen or India ink pen. Prepare screen by mixing 2 teaspoons photo emulsion with ½ teaspoon sensitizer in a disposable cup. Mixture will turn green. Pour mixture on the bottom side of the screen and spread evenly with ink spreader or a stiff piece of cardboard. Place screen in a dark place (in a box, closet or drawer) and allow to dry for approximately 20-30 minutes. While screen is drying, set up your light source. Cut a hole in the aluminum pie plate, fit it on the light socket and screw on the #1 photo flood bulb. Place black paper 10" to 12" under your light source on a flat surface (table, counter, floor, etc.). Remove dry screen from dark area and place it on the black paper, bottom side of screen down. Place tracing paper design on the screen in the position you want your stencil; secure the edges with cellophane tape or cover entire design with a piece of glass or plexiglass to assure total contact. Turn on the light, wait 10 minutes, turn light off. Remove the pattern from screen. Wash screen on both sides under cool running water. Screen is completely clean when you can see through it. Allow screen to dry thoroughly. When dry, check the screen for any pin holes. Fill unwanted holes with screen filler. Place the screen on the area of the chest to be printed; make registration marks with a soft lead pencil, lining up elephant trunks with tails. Print the dark blue elephants first. Apply ink across the top of the screen, press down on the screen with one hand; with the squeegee, push the ink downward over the screen in one even stroke; push excess ink back to the top of the screen, maintaining even pressure. Lift screen from chest and design is printed. (Stencil can be used for approximately 75 printings.) When blue elephants are completed, clean blue ink from screen with water. Allow screen to dry and repeat printing process with orange ink. Wash out

orange ink and allow screen to dry. Place dry screen on a piece of paper with child's name. Copy name onto open area of elephant with soft lead pencil. Paint in name with screen filler; allow to dry. Print elephant with name where desired. To dissolve stencil, mix one part bleach and two parts water; rinse out with warm water. Let screen dry and repeat process for additional stencils.

RUFFLED APPLIQUE PILLOWS

(pages 84 and 86)

MATERIALS—For Rooster, Hen, Wreath, and Bowl and Pitcher pillows: Solid fabric, 16½" square and a strip (can be pieced) 5⅝" x 123"; thread to match; printed fabric, 16½" square and a strip 3⅝" x 123"; thread to match; fabric scraps for appliqué; thread to match; one bag of polyester fiberfill for each pillow; pencil; paper for patterns; white glue; Stitch Witchery® fusible webbing; scissors; pins. **For Strawberry pillow:** Solid fabric, two 16½" squares and a strip 7" x 123"; thread to match; fabric scraps for appliqué; thread to match; green thread for vines; one bag of polyester fiberfill; pencil; paper for patterns; white glue; Stitch Witchery® fusible webbing; scissors; pins.

ROOSTER PILLOW   1 SQ.=1"

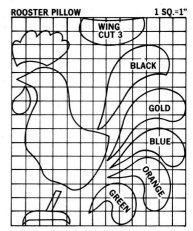

WING CUT 3
BLACK
GOLD
BLUE
ORANGE
GREEN

DIRECTIONS—For Rooster, Hen, Wreath, and Bowl and Pitcher pillows: Following directions on page 37 enlarge appliqué pattern and trace onto paper. Cut out pattern pieces and trace onto fabrics. Cut out. Using photo and pattern as guides, form design on solid square of fabric, keeping pieces in place with a dab of white glue. Working one piece at a time, attach pieces together and to solid fabric square, following Stitch Witchery® directions. For stitching down appliqués with a zigzag sewing machine, set the length of the stitches very close to give the effect of satin stitching, using photo and pattern as guides. Stitch over all raw edges; press appliqué smooth. If necessary, piece

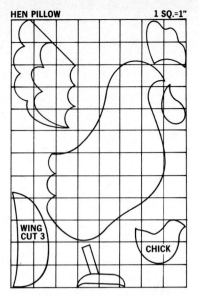

HEN PILLOW   1 SQ.=1"

WING CUT 3

CHICK

long strips of solid and print fabrics with ½" seams; press seams to one side. With right sides together, stitch solid strip to print strip with a ½" seam along one long edge. Trim seam to ¼"; press toward solid strip. Fold wrong sides together with raw edges even; press along fold to leave 1" border of solid fabric as shown. With right sides together, stitch ½" seams in short ends of strip; turn; press. Baste raw edges together with long machine stitches, ⅜" from edge; stitch again ¼" from previous stitching.

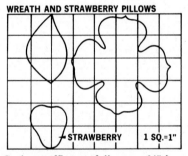

WREATH AND STRAWBERRY PILLOWS

STRAWBERRY   1 SQ.=1"

Gather ruffle carefully to a 64" long strip. Pin ruffle to appliquéd square, right sides together, overlapping 2" of ruffle at bottom of square. Stitch ruffle to square, just inside second row of gathering stitches. With ruffle still toward appliquéd square, pin right side of print fabric to right side of appliquéd square, keeping ruffle free. Stitch a ½" seam through all thicknesses on three sides; turn and press, pressing ruffle away from squares. Stuff with polyester fiberfill until firm;

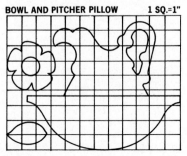

BOWL AND PITCHER PILLOW   1 SQ.=1"

---

fold ½" under on free edge of back square and whipstitch opening closed, tucking in seam allowance of ruffle and front square. **For Strawberry pillow:** Follow directions for other pillows, with the following changes: Do not use Stitch Witchery® to attach appliqué to solid fabric square. Instead, stitch partially around each strawberry, leaving a small opening at the top. With a pencil point or other narrow object, stuff a small amount of polyester fiberfill into each strawberry to pad it, then finish stitching around. Do not press appliquéd design. To make ruffle, fold solid fabric strip in half lengthwise; stitch ½" seams in both short ends and continue following directions for other pillows.

NATURAL BEAN LAMP

(page 84)

MATERIALS: Photographer's reflector lamp shade (about 12" in diameter); screw-in light bulb socket to fit shade; white swag lamp chain and screw-in eye to attach chain to socket; about 15 feet of white electrical cord (figure length by measuring length from lamp to ceiling, across ceiling to wall, and down wall to rug); snap-on switch and plug for cord; heavy-duty sky hook; antique white spray paint; Scotch Super Strength Adhesive®; Scotchgard® fabric protector; ¼ pound each: red lentils, green lentils, green split peas, yellow split peas, mung beans, cracked wheat, and millet (if not available in supermarkets, try health food stores).
DIRECTIONS: Screw light bulb socket into photographer's lamp shade. Wire socket with electrical cord. Screw chain into top of socket and thread cord through chain links. Spray lamp inside and out with white spray paint. Use at least 2 coats to get even coverage, letting paint dry thoroughly between coats. Place each type of bean in a separate bowl to make handling easier. Spread newspaper under work surface. With a pencil, lightly sketch a pattern on lamp to follow when gluing down beans and seeds. The pattern needn't be exact. Refer to the photo on page 84 as a guide, if you wish. Working on one small area at a time, from bottom up, apply Super Strength Adhesive® liberally to lamp and pour a handful of one type of bean or seed onto glued area. Use enough glue to embed beans and push them into place as you go. Following your pattern, continue to spiral beans and seeds up neck of lamp. When lamp is completely covered, allow to dry at least 24 hours, then gently shake lamp to remove loose beans. Repair any bare spots and allow to dry. Spray

---

surface with Scotchgard® fabric protector. Install sky hook in ceiling. Hook chain to sky hook at desired level. Run cord across ceiling and down wall to electrical outlet; attach plug to end of cord. Attach switch at convenient height, following manufacturer's directions.

BATIK ACCESSORIES

(page 85)

MATERIALS: Bleached muslin or 100% cotton white sheets; polyester batting; wooden stretcher frame; push pins; fine natural bristle brush or tjanting tool; double boiler; batik wax or plain white candles; Rit dyes in desired colors; iron; white paper towels; iron fusible web; paper for pattern; black felt-tipped pen; pencil.

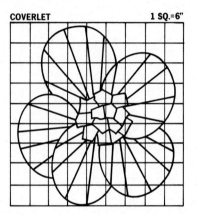

COVERLET   1 SQ.=6"

DIRECTIONS: All items are simple "easy batiks" requiring one waxing and one dyeing. Select designs from those given. For the pillows, we varied sizes from 12" to 18" in diameter for contrast. The coverlet is 54" in diameter. The 12 leaves for the lamp shade should extend a few inches below bottom edge of shade. The number and size leaves you will need are determined by the size and shape of the lamp shade. We used 19" leaves. Wash and dry fabric first to remove excess sizing. Following directions on page 37, enlarge designs onto paper using a black felt-tipped pen. Trace design *very* lightly in pencil onto fabric. **(For lamp shade leaves and coverlet only:** Stitch a fine zigzag stitch ¼" from outside edge. After waxing and dyeing are complete, cut away excess fabric close to stitching line, leaving a finished edge.) Once all the designs are sketched onto the fabric, you're ready to batik. Place wax in top half of double boiler. Fill bottom half with

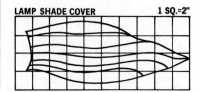

LAMP SHADE COVER   1 SQ.=2"

PILLOW 1 SQ.=2"

about 1½" water and place over low heat. (**Note:** If using your stovetop, tape a piece of aluminum foil on stove edge to protect it from drips.) Keep water simmering throughout waxing procedure, being sure to add more

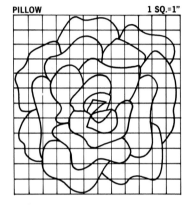

PILLOW 1 SQ.=1"

water as it evaporates. Allow at least 35 minutes for wax to liquify. When wax is ready (it should look like slightly tinted or translucent water) dip brush in wax for a few seconds and dab a bit on scrap fabric. Turn fabric to other side to be sure that wax

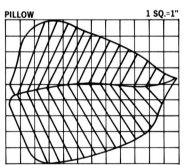

PILLOW 1 SQ.=1"

has penetrated completely. If not, heat wax several minutes more and test again. Never heat wax directly over heat source; if it begins to smoke, remove from heat immediately. Stretch fabric on stretcher frame using

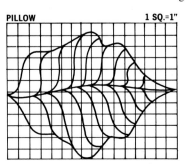

PILLOW 1 SQ.=1"

push pins to keep it taut. Brush on wax following sketched lines. A tjanting tool gives a longer "stroke," but it may be easier to work with a fine brush. Wax cools and hardens seconds after it touches fabric, so it's best to work in short, careful brush strokes to make sure wax is penetrating fabric fully. If wax does not go through to other side, turn fabric over and touch up missed spots. Fabric is now ready to be died. Follow Rit® package instructions *except* make sure water temperature is warm, *not* hot, since hot water will melt wax. For the leaves, we used Avocado and 1 part Gold mixed with 1 part Avocado. For the flowers, we used Coral, Old Rose and 5 parts Fuschia mixed with 1 part Royal. (**Note:** The backing for pillows may be purchased separately or dyed to match, using additonal muslin or sheeting.) Hang fabric on clothes line to dry (*never* put waxed fabric in a dryer or near a heater). **To remove wax:** Place batik pieces between layers of white paper toweling and use medium-hot iron to melt wax. Change paper towels often so that wax in towels won't transfer to next piece. You will notice a dark line next to the white batiked area—this is wax that will be difficult to remove completely unless you dry clean the item. Often it is desirable to leave this excess wax in the item as it adds contrast. **To finish—Pillows:** Stitch front and back sections of each pillow together, right sides facing. Leave a 3"-4" opening for stuffing. Turn right side out. Stuff with batting. Hand stitch closed. **Coverlet:** Trim close to stitching for finished edge. **Lamp shade Cover:** Trim edges close to stitching line for finished look. Arrange leaves around lamp shade until you achieve adequate spacing. Then, taking one leaf at a time, use fusible web to attach one to another. Continue adding leaves and refitting on lampshade until a full circle is made. Tuck hanging ends under shade; glue or tape.

GROW CHART WALL HANGING

(page 85)

MATERIALS: Phun Phelt® in the following colors and sizes: 2 yds. white, ¼ yd. brown, ¼ yd. dark green, one 9"x12" piece dark blue, one 9"x12" piece orange, two 9"x12" pieces rose, two 9"x12" pieces light green, two 9"x12" pieces yellow; 2½ yds. Pellon fusible webbing; Slomon's Velverette Craft Glue; rug tape; paper for patterns; pencil; iron; yardstick; pressing cloth; scissors; scrap cardboard of tissue box weight.

DIRECTIONS: Choose a large, flat surface on which to work. Cut 2 pieces white Phelt® 6'x2'. Sandwich fusible

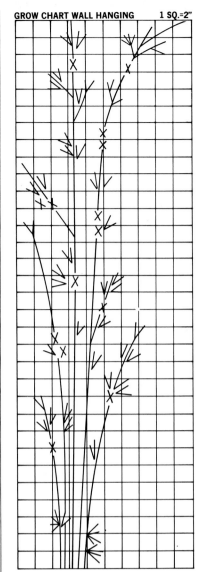

GROW CHART WALL HANGING 1 SQ.=2"

webbing between the pieces, using the extra ½ yd. to piece out the necessary width. Bond according to manufacturer's directions. Following directions on page 37, enlarge and cut out paper patterns for flower, leaf, bird and turtle. (Cut out flower pattern along broken line.) Cut out entire turtle pattern of dark green Phelt®. Then cut pattern apart to give pat-

GROW CHART WALL HANGING 1 SQ.=1"

terns for interior markings on shell. Cut these of light green. Glue to turtle. When gluing small pieces, use strips of tissue box (or similar) cardboard to apply glue. Cut strips about 2½″x¼″. Discard these frequently. For larger areas, use flat edge of larger piece of cardboard as spatula to smooth glue thinly. Finish turtle with thin strip for mouth and round dot for eye, both of light green Phelt®; set aside. Using pattern, cut 13 leaves of light green and 41 of dark green Phelt®; set aside. Cut out 10 rose and 5 orange flowers. Cut pattern down to inner petal edge. Cut 15 of yellow, using this pattern. Glue yellow flower to each of the rose and orange flowers. Cut pattern down to star. Cut 15 of light green and glue one in center of each flower. Cut 10 rose and 5 orange round centers. Glue to center of flower of same color. Set all aside. Following directions on page 119, make paper pattern for position of stems, leaves and flowers. Lightly mark white Phelt® hanging according to your pattern. Using this as a guide, glue flowers in place, gluing them at centers only. (All pairs are of one rose and one orange.) Cut brown stems ¼″ wide and fit in place, tucking ends under petals. Taper stem ends at tips. Make side branches slightly narrower. Glue leaves as indicated, mixing light and dark as shown. Cut bird pattern apart and use to cut dark blue head, wings and tail with rose breast. Feet and eye are yellow and beak is orange. Glue in place on branch. Glue turtle as shown. Mark inches and feet along right edge of hanging. Cut ⅛″ wide strips of blue. Cut these into ½″ long pieces for inch marks and 1″ pieces for foot marks. Glue in place. Following directions on page 37, enlarge and cut out patterns for numbers. Cut out numbers from blue Phelt®. Glue in place next to foot marks. Hang chart with double-faced rug tape.

RECORD TABLE

(page 86)

MATERIALS: Fir—4 legs 3″x3″x28″ (A), 2 ends 1¼″x3″x8″ (B), 2 sides 1¼″x3″x31″ (C), 4 (45°) angle pieces 1¼″x1¼″x6½″ (D), 2 side runners 1″x1″x25″ (E), 2 front racks ¼″x6″x36″ lattice (F), 2 back racks ¼″x6″x36″ lattice (G), 2 back runners ¼″x1¼″x31″ lattice (H), 8 dividers ¼″x6″x13″ lattice (I), 2 end braces 1½″x1½″x6″ (J), 2 side braces 1½″x1½″x36″ (K); birch plywood—1 table top ¾″x10-⅞″x35-9/16 (L); white glue; 1¼″ wood screws; 1″ wire nails; pipe clamp.

DIRECTIONS: Using glue and clamps, assemble legs (A) to ends (B). Assemble legs (A) to sides (C) in the same way. Glue and screw angle pieces (D) to (B) and (C), ¾″ down. Glue and screw side runners (E) ¾″ down on sides (C), mitering corners at a 45° angle. Notch table top (L) 1⅝″ to fit. Screw table top in place from side runners (E). Notch front rack pieces (F) 2½″x2¼″ to fit legs also. Glue and nail back runners (H) to back racks (G). Glue and nail dividers (I) to racks (F) and (G). Turn table upside down and position the racks in place. Screw braces (J) and (K) in place. Turn table right side up. Glue and nail racks to legs and runners. Sand and wax.

RECORD TABLE

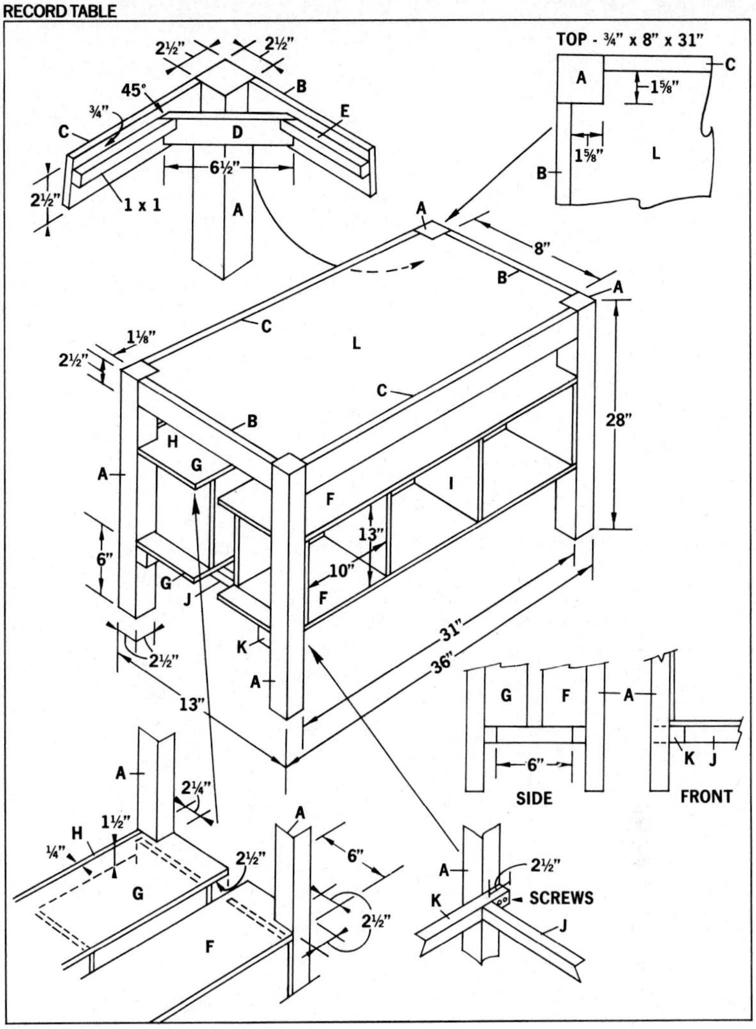
TOP - ¾″ x 8″ x 31″
45°
2½″
¾″
6½″
1 x 1
1⅝″
8″
28″
13″
10″
6″
31″
36″
SIDE
FRONT
SCREWS
H
G
F
L
A
B
C
D
E
I
J
K

PARQUET DINING TABLE

(page 86)

MATERIALS: Four 4″x4″x29½″ legs; four 1½″x3½″x29″ cross pieces; one 1½″x2½″x72″ stretcher; 36″x72″ flakeboard top; two 1″x3″ wedges tapered to ½″x3″; two 1½″x3½″ top end pieces; two 2″x3″ end pieces; ¾″ pine apron for top; Hartco Wood Flor-Tile® in natural standard oak; Wilhold Aliphatic Resin Wood Glue; drill; chisel; medium sandpaper; sealer; varnish.

DIRECTIONS: Cut four legs 4″x4″x29½″. Cut notches 1½″x3½″ at points indicated in diagram. Cut four cross pieces 1½″x3½″x29″. With drill and chisel, cut one mortise ¾″x2¾″ in the center of each lower cross piece. Cut one stretcher 1½″x2½″x72″. Cut 3½″ deep shoulder 3½″ from each end of stretcher. Chisel waste to form a tongue ¾″x2½″; round end. Cut a mortise ¾″x1″ at a point 1⅜″ from shoulder. Cut two wedges for this mortise, 1″x3″

PARQUET DINING TABLE

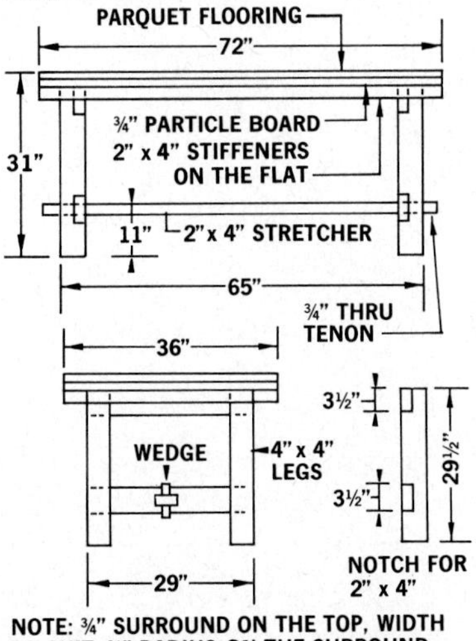
PARQUET FLOORING
72″
¾″ PARTICLE BOARD
2″ x 4″ STIFFENERS ON THE FLAT
31″
11″
2″x 4″ STRETCHER
65″
¾″ THRU TENON
36″
3½″
WEDGE
4″ x 4″ LEGS
3½″
29½″
29″
NOTCH FOR 2″ x 4″

NOTE: ¾″ SURROUND ON THE TOP, WIDTH TO SUIT. ⅜″ RADIUS ON THE SURROUND

tapered to ½"x3". Glue and nail cross pieces to legs. Push tenon (on stretcher) through the mortise in the lower stretcher and drive wedges up tight. Cut one flakeboard top 36"x72" and nail one 1½"x3½" on each end. Place on top of uprights and nail down into legs and cross pieces. Cut and nail two 2"x3"'s between legs and into top. Cut ¾" pine apron for top with a ⅜" radius wide enough to cover 2"x3", ¾" flakeboard and edge of parquet. Trim edges of parquet and glue to flakeboard. Sand, seal and varnish all raw wood.

TOILET PAPER HOLDER

(page 86)

MATERIALS: One ½" x 8" x 5" plywood for back (A); two 1½" x 5" x 6" fir or pine for sides (B); one dowel or bamboo piece, 1½" in diameter and 5½" long; chisel; mallet or hammer; 1⅝" bit and drill; two 1" hinges; two friction catches; ruler; pencil; black paint and brush or cotton swab for application, or black felt-tipped marker; fine sandpaper; 000 gauge steel wool; Minwax wood stain in color of your choice; polyurethane finish; brushes for application; two screws for mounting; screwdriver.

TOILET ROLL HOLDER

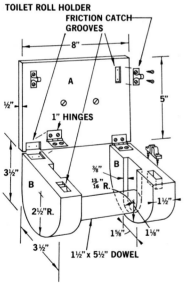

DIRECTIONS—Preparing Wood: Cut out one A and two B pieces (see diagram). Using drill and 1⅝" bit, drill a ⅜"-deep hole in each B piece; note the center is 1⅛" from arc and the radius is 13/16". Chisel grooves to meet the holes. Chisel 2 shallow rectangular grooves on bottom of A and 2 on bottom of each B, so hinges will lie flush with surface (see diagram). Chisel a rectangular hole to hold clip part of friction catch in each B (only strike part of catch should lie above surface of B when catch is closed). **Assembling:** Screw hinges and clip of catches into their respective

grooves. To determine where to attach strikes on A, stick strikes into clips already attached to B. Dab a bit of black paint or felt-tipped marker ink on backs of strikes; swing both B's up to, and touching, A. These are the exact points for positioning the strikes. Chisel rectangular grooves into wood so that strikes will lie flush with surface (see diagram); screw strikes into A. Test for mobility to make sure everything fits properly. **Staining:** Sand surfaces of A and both B's smooth with sandpaper. Wet wood and allow to dry; give a final sanding with steel wool. Paint with one coat of wood stain, then 3 coats of polyurethane finish, sanding between each coat with steel wool. **Finishing:** Leave dowel unvarnished, to better grip toilet paper roll. Drill 2 holes in A and countersink screws for mounting.

ARCHED MIRROR

(page 87)

MATERIALS: ½"-thick plywood, 18"x30"; saber saw; dime-store mirror, 8"x12"; 1 quart Grumbacher Hyplar® Modeling Paste; Rit® Liquid Dye in the following colors (1 bottle each): Marine Blue, Evening Blue, Olive Green, Yellow; Krylon® High Gloss Spray Varnish; medium-fine sandpaper; pencil; string; ruler; plastic drop cloth; kitchen knife and fork for modeling; pastry tube; sponge; white latex paint; paint brush; Elmer's Glue-All®; masking tape; four ½" flat hinges.

DIRECTIONS: Cut 1 piece plywood 12"x16½" for central panel; 2 pieces 8"x14½" for side panels. Sand edges lightly. To draw the arches on top, attach a string to a pencil and adjust the string length so that from the center of the board the pencil just touches sides and top. Draw the arch; cut with saber saw. To draw outline for mirror hole, measure in 3 inches all around on central panel; cut with saber saw. Hole will measure 6"x10½". Sand edges lightly. Lay pieces flat on plastic drop cloth. Apply Hyplar® Modeling Paste with knife to ½" thickness, on one side only. Use the knife to create swirls; use the fork to create scallops and lines. Fill pastry tube with modeling paste and apply final flourishes. Allow to dry overnight or until thoroughly dry. Surface will look like crisp plaster. Pour a small amount of dye in saucer and dilute with water to lighten. Apply to panels with a sponge, using easy, sweeping strokes for a light tint. To create deep tones, pour small amount of diluted dye directly onto panel in puddles. Allow to dry thoroughly. Salt residue will

remain, creating a salt glaze look. To change colors or to correct mistakes, paint out color with white latex and dye again. When thoroughly dry, give panels 3 coats of Krylon® High Gloss Varnish. Allow each coat to dry thoroughly before applying the next. Turn panels over and apply a thin coat of modeling paste to the other side with a knife. Spread over the entire surface, including edges, to create a stucco look. Allow to dry several hours. When thoroughly dry, apply 1 coat of white latex paint. When dry, spray with varnish. Glue mirror to back of frame. Apply masking tape to hold mirror firmly against frame while glue dries overnight. Remove tape. Attach flat hinges to connect panels.

POSY SLING CHAIR

(page 87)

MATERIALS: Samsonite Body Glove Folding Sling Chair (see Buyer's Guide, page 120); 3-ply tapestry wool in the following colors and amounts: ½ ounce each of dark blue, light green, dark green and yellow, 1 ounce of light blue; size 18 tapestry needle; thimble; Scotchgard® fabric

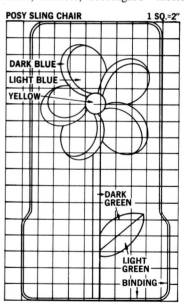

protector; white paper for pattern.
DIRECTIONS: Following directions on page 37, enlarge pattern onto white paper. Transfer the design onto the sling (it will easily slide off the frame.) To needlepoint, be sure to work with one hand between the layers to prevent catching the back of the sling. Using a thimble, work the design following this guide (see Needlepoint Stitch guide, page 128): Yellow and dark blue, basketweave stitch. (**Note:** Do *not* use a continental stitch as it will stretch the canvas out of shape); light blue, diamond stitch; dark green, brick stitch; light green, horizontal brick stitch. When design

is finished, carefully clip all loose threads and spray front of chair with Scotchgard®. Replace sling on frame.

VILLAGE FLOOR GAME

(page 87)

MATERIALS: ½"-thick plywood, 36"x36"; medium-fine sandpaper; 1 quart flat white latex paint; 1 pint Grumbacher Hyplar® Matte Medium Varnish; Grumbacher Hyplar® Acrylic Paints in the following colors: Red HO95, Black H134, Crimson H204, Green H162, Blue H203, Orange H099, White H212, Yellow H031; paint brushes, one each size 6 and size 8, one 2" wide; masking tape; large sheet of brown wrapping paper for pattern; tracing paper; pencil; scissors; Krylon® High Gloss Varnish.

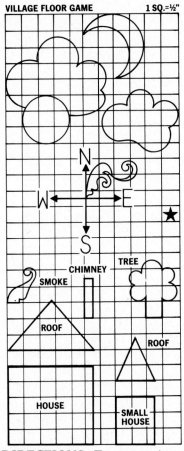

VILLAGE FLOOR GAME   1 SQ.=½"

DIRECTIONS: To prepare board, sand edges smooth and give both sides 2 coats of white latex paint. Following directions on page 37, enlarge road pattern onto brown paper. Rub wrong side of pattern with a pencil. Tape pattern in place on board, wrong side down; trace. Remove pattern. (Pencil lines should be visible on board; if not, repeat, pressing down harder.) Trace houses, trees, smoke, roofs, compass, moon, stars and clouds onto tracing paper. Transfer patterns to game board, referring to photo for placement. (**Note:** Town

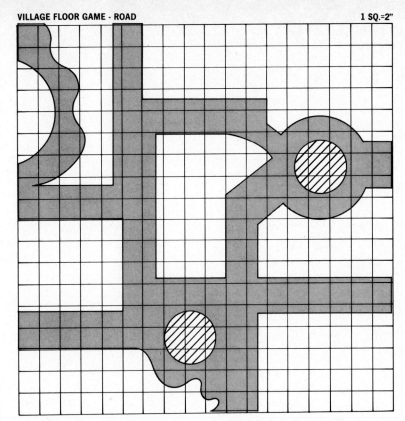

VILLAGE FLOOR GAME - ROAD   1 SQ.=2"

Hall is a combination of large house base and small house roof.)

To mix paints: Thin paints with a small amount of water to consistency of heavy cream. Apply several thin coats for durability and a solid, opaque look. Clean brushes with soap and water. The colors used in painting the village were mixed to create stronger, brighter hues: Orange into Yellow = Yellow; Orange into Red = Red; Yellow into Green = Green; Blue and Crimson into White = Lavender.

To paint: Tape all straight lines, keeping road open. Before painting, seal with a light coat of Hyplar Matte Medium Varnish. (This saves hours of fussy touching up when you peel tape off.) Allow varnish to dry thoroughly. Paint road Black, allowing each coat to dry thoroughly before applying the next. Remove tape carefully. Paint park circle Green. Tape around each house base and seal with varnish. Allow to dry thoroughly before painting house bases in your choice of colors. When paint is thoroughly dry, remove tape carefully. Next, tape around roofs and chimneys. Paint these Black. Paint trees Green. Paint smoke, compass, clouds, moon and stars in your choice of colors. When board is completely finished and paint is thoroughly dry, remove all tape carefully. Clean up smudges and spray entire board with 3 coats of Krylon® High Gloss Varnish. Be sure to allow each coat of varnish to dry overnight before applying the next.

ROSE PRINT DESIGNS

(page 87)

MATERIALS: Hunt/Speedball Fabric Screen Printing Kit (or: 10"x14" screen, stiff piece of cardboard, squeegee, 4 oz. Hunt/Speedball photo emulsion, 1 oz. Hunt/Speedball sensitizer, 4 oz. Hunt/Speedball screen filler, tracing paper, small artist's paint brush); 1 qt. Hunt/Speedball white textile ink: 8 oz. each, green, brown and yellow Hunt/Speedball textile ink; black felt-tipped or India ink pen; cellophane tape; #1 photo flood light bulb; lamp cord with standard socket; disposable cup; sheet of black paper; 10"-12" aluminum pie plate; soft lead pencil; ruler; masking tape; chlorine bleach; Deacon's Bench from Sears, #1H 12291L; 5 yds. cotton duck; fiberfill; 4'x6' carpet remnant.

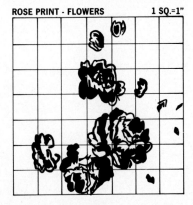

ROSE PRINT - FLOWERS   1 SQ.=1"

DIRECTIONS: Following directions on page 37, enlarge floral motif onto tracing paper. Make one pattern for the flower, another for the stems. Fill in the areas to be printed with a black felt-tipped or India ink pen. You will have to make a stencil for each color. You can use one screen, or if you have two, prepare both with the emulsion/sensitizer mixture.

ROSE PRINT · STEMS   **1 SQ.=1"**

To make stencil: Prepare screen by mixing 2 teaspoons photo emulsion with ½ teaspoon sensitizer in a disposable cup. Mixture will turn green. Pour mixture on the bottom side of the screen and spread evenly with ink spreader or a stiff piece of cardboard. Place screen in a dark place (in a box, closet or drawer) and allow to dry for approximately 20-30 minutes. While screen is drying, set up your light source. Cut a hole in the aluminum pie plate, fit it on the light socket and screw on the #1 photo flood bulb. Place black paper 10" to 12" under your light source on a flat surface (table, counter, floor, etc.). Remove dry screen from dark area and place it on the black paper, bottom side of screen down. Place tracing paper design, flower pattern only, on the screen in the position you want your stencil; secure the edges with cellophane tape or cover entire design with a piece of glass or plexiglass to assure total contact. Turn on the light, wait 10 minutes, turn light off. Remove pattern from screen. Wash screen on both sides under cool running water. Screen is completely clean when you can see through it. Allow screen to dry thoroughly. When dry, check screen for any pin holes. Fill unwanted holes with screen filler. **To prepare fabric, carpet and bench:** With pencil or tailor's chalk, draw horizontal and vertical lines on the right side of the fabric, forming blocks measuring 8"x11". Make corresponding marks on the screen frame. Tape or pin fabric to a flat surface to prevent

movement. Make registration marks on deacon's bench. For the carpet, make your registration marks with pieces of masking tape. **To mix colors:** To mix the rose color, start with ½ qt. white textile ink and add 2 tablespoons red, 1 tablespoon brown and 1 tablespoon yellow. To mix the green, start with ½ qt. white textile ink and add 4 tablespoons green, 1 tablespoon brown and 1 tablespoon yellow. **To print:** Print all the rose colored areas first. Place the screen on the area of the fabric, carpet or bench to be printed, lining up registration marks. Apply ink across the top of the screen, press down on the screen with one hand; with the squeegee, push the ink downward over the screen in one even stroke; push excess ink back to the top of the screen, maintaining even pressure. Lift screen, and design is printed. (Stencil can be used for approximately 75 printings.) Continue to print, skipping every other box. When you've finished printing all the roses, wash screen clean with water. If you have only one screen, dissolve rose stencil by mixing 1 part chlorine bleach with 2 parts water; pour on screen, let stand for 4 minutes and wash screen with warm water. Follow instructions for making a stencil, this time using the stem pattern. Place dry, prepared screen on fabric, carpet or bench which has been printed with the rose pattern. Your first color print will be visible through the screen's coating so you can align the tracing paper pattern with the print below for the perfect color registration. Secure the pattern to the screen with tape in desired position. After the second stencil is complete, print the green stems. **To complete:** When fabric has dried, heat set it for washability by ironing it for 3 to 5 minutes, or throw it in the clothes dryer for 30 minutes. Your fabric can now be washed or dry cleaned. Cut fabric to desired dimensions for pillows. Sew together, right sides facing, leaving an opening for stuffing. Turn right side out; stuff; whipstitch closed.

FLORAL WALL HANGING

(page 87)

MATERIALS: Phun Phelt® in the following colors and sizes: 2½ yds. white, ¼ yd. yellow, ¼ yd. rose, ⅛ yd. light green, ⅛ yd. dark green, one 9"x12" piece aqua; 6 yds. Pellon fusible webbing; Slomon's Velverette Craft Glue; dark green knitting worsted; thread to match; rug tape for hanging; paper for patterns; pencil; scissors; yardstick; iron; pressing cloth; scrap cardboard of tissue box weight.

FLORAL WALL HANGING CUTTING DIAGRAM

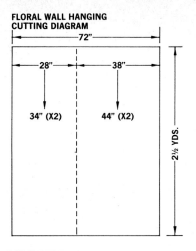

DIRECTIONS: Following cutting diagram, cut two 28"x34½" pieces white Phelt®. Sandwich fusible webbing between the pieces. Fuse, following manufacturer's directions. Cut two 38"x44½" pieces white Phelt® and fuse together, following manufacturer's directions. Center smaller fused on larger one and glue both together. Cut ⅝"-wide strips of rose Phelt®, two 44½" and two 38". These will make the outer frame. Trim corners to fit and glue in place on outer edge of larger fused piece. Cut ½"-wide strips of rose Phelt®, two 29" and two 35½", to make the inner frame. Trim corners to fit and glue in place on the larger fused piece, adjacent to edge of smaller piece. They are glued around the inner piece, not on it. Following directions on page 37, enlarge patterns showing placement of vine, basket, leaves, flowers and berries. Use these patterns as a guide to make very light marks on the white Phelt®. Following directions on page 37,

FLORAL WALL HANGING   **1 SQ.=2"**

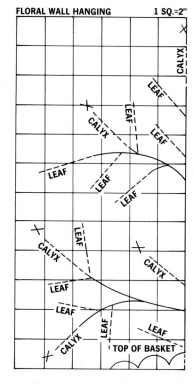

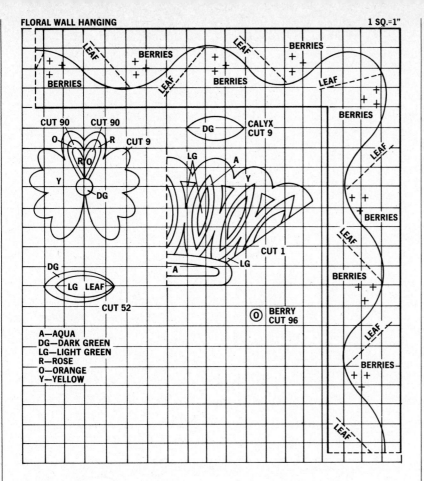

FLORAL WALL HANGING

1 SQ.=1"

LEAF
BERRIES
LEAF
BERRIES
BERRIES
LEAF
LEAF
BERRIES

CUT 90 CUT 90
CUT 9
O   R
R/O
Y
DG

DG
CALYX
CUT 9

LG
A
Y
A

CUT 1
LG
A
LG

DG
LG LEAF
CUT 52

BERRIES

BERRIES
LEAF
BERRIES

O BERRY
CUT 96

LEAF
BERRIES

A—AQUA
DG—DARK GREEN
LG—LIGHT GREEN
R—ROSE
O—ORANGE
Y—YELLOW

LEAF

enlarge and cut out patterns for leaves, basket, flowers, berries and calyx. Cut out shapes in appropriate color Phelt®. Berries are one layer of orange; calyx, one layer of dark green. Leaves are full size dark green, with smaller light green leaf glued on. Flowers are made of full yellow background with two layers of orange and rose hearts glued on each petal. Centers are dark green. Basket is yellow, light green and aqua. Glue all in their proper location, following the pattern. Cut small strips of scrap cardboard (about 2½″x¼″) and use like tiny spatulas to spread glue over Phelt®. All stems and vine are simple three-strand braids, using three strands of knitting worsted for each braid. Make them as long as is practical to manage. Tie ends invisibly with matching sewing thread. Glue along marked lines. Use double-faced rug tape to hang, or glue narrow wooden strips to top and bottom of back and use tiny screw eyes and hooks to hang.

CUSTOMIZED PLYWOOD SCREENS

(page 88)

MATERIALS: One 4′x8′ sheet of ½″ APA grade-trademarked A-C, A-D or MDO plywood; 12 pieces 1″x3″x6′ dado (not necessary for graphic design screen); 3 pairs 1½″ double-

acting hinges (butt hinges or continuous hinge may have to be substituted because of availability); white glue; finishing nails; wood putty or spackle; sandpaper.

PLYWOOD SCREENS

1½″ 1½″ 1½″ 1½″ ½″

12″ x 12″ MIRROR TILES
CEDAR STRIP
60″

15″ 15″ 15″ ½″

NOTE: TRY TO MATCH COLOR OF CEDAR STRIP WITH 1 x 3

DIRECTIONS: To build one of the screens, simply cut your sheet of plywood into three 15″x60″ pieces. You might be able to have this done where you buy the plywood. (If you're painting the screen with graphics or the Pennsylvania Dutch motif shown here, use MDO, Medium Overlaid Density, plywood. Overlaid with a resin-treated fiber, this plywood is

smooth and extremely easy to paint.) Fill the edges of plywood with wood putty or spackle; sand lightly; hinge the panels together. If you're using butt or continuous hinges, remember to alternate the direction of the second and third hinges so the screen will unfold properly.

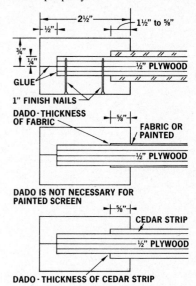

2½″
½″ 1½″ to ⅝″
¾″
¼″
½″ PLYWOOD
GLUE
1″ FINISH NAILS
DADO-THICKNESS OF FABRIC
⅝″
FABRIC OR PAINTED
½″ PLYWOOD
DADO IS NOT NECESSARY FOR PAINTED SCREEN
⅝″
CEDAR STRIP
½″ PLYWOOD
DADO-THICKNESS OF CEDAR STRIP

Mirror Tile Screen: You will need thirty 12″x12″ mirror tiles to cover both sides of a three-panel screen. Attach tiles with the recommended adhesive and then glue and nail 1″x3″ dado, as shown in diagram, to cover tile edges and help hold tiles in place.

Wood Panel Screen: Many different types of wood are available in these thin strips that can be cut with ordinary scissors and applied with panel adhesive. Each package of strips covers about 33 square feet, so you'll need about a package and a half to cover both sides of a three-panel screen. Glue and nail 1″x3″ dado to screen as shown in diagram.

PLYWOOD SCREEN GRAPHICS

1 SQ.=4″

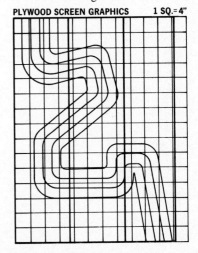

Graphic Design Screen: Paint plywood screens white. Following directions on page 37, enlarge graphic design onto paper. Trace pattern onto plywood panels. Paint designs with acrylic paints, using masking tape to guide the design lines. Use the photo on page 88 as a color guide or use any colors that will complement your decorating scheme. Paint one color at a time, allowing each to dry thoroughly before painting the next. Glue and nail 1″x3″ dado to screen as shown in diagram.

PLYWOOD SCREENS - PENNSYLVANIA DUTCH MOTIF 1 SQ.= 2″

Pennsylvania Dutch Screen: Paint plywood screens white. Following directions on page 37, enlarge design for Pennsylvania Dutch Motif onto paper. Cut out pattern and trace onto plywood panels. Paint motif with acrylic paints, using the photo on page 88 as a color guide. (Paints may have to be thinned slightly with a small amount of water.) If a darker color is desired, more paint can be added when the first coat of acrylic has dried. Glue and nail 1″x3″ dado to screen as shown in diagram.

WOOL STITCHERY BOUQUET

(page 87)

Finished size measures 18″x24″.
MATERIALS: 22″x28″ piece of 13-mesh mono canvas (larger or smaller mesh canvas will mean different size piece); masking tape (to edge canvas); size 18 tapestry needle; permanent ink felt-tipped markers; pencil; white paper for pattern; 3-ply 100% wool yarns in the following colors and amounts (**Note:** Yarn amounts listed are for 13-mesh mono canvas): ½ ounce each of light yellow, yellow, pale violet, light violet, medium violet, dark violet, light peach, peach, light rose, rose, pale pink, light pink, medium pink, dark pink, light turquoise, dark turquoise, light slate blue, medium slate blue, dark slate blue, light green, medium green, yellow green, light olive, medium olive, dark olive; 2 ounces of pale green. **To finish:** 18″x24″ wood canvas stretchers; staple gun or hammer and carpet tacks; frame, as desired.

DIRECTIONS: Following directions on page 37, enlarge pattern onto white paper. Mark outlines with heavy pencil line or felt-tipped marker. Tape edge of canvas. Mark 18″x24″ outline, leaving 2″ border on each side. Position pattern under canvas, centering it in the outline. Trace design onto canvas with felt-tipped marker. Work the design, using the Needlecraft Stitch Guide, page 128, if necessary. **Flowers:** The center of daffodil and rose are French knots; pink carnations are done with long and short stitch; violets, tulips, rose and daffodil are all worked in the basketweave stitch. **Leaves:** Leaves are worked in a random combination of brick, basketweave, diagonal mosaic, mosaic and Parisian stitches. **Stems:** Stem stitch. **Background:** Basketweave with a satin stitch border. **To finish:** If no frame is used, block canvas, either professionally or using blocking kit. If frame is used, there is no need to block canvas. Mark top and side centers on canvas and stretcher strips. Assemble stretcher corners. Use center lines on canvas to match marks on stretcher and tack or staple needlepoint in place; pull taut, alternating on all 4 sides until piece is evenly stretched.

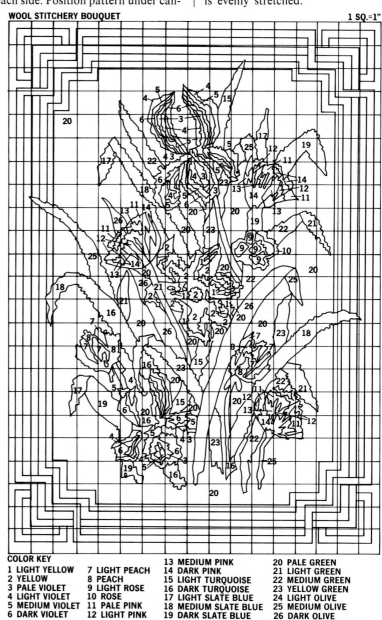

WOOL STITCHERY BOUQUET 1 SQ.=1″

COLOR KEY

1 LIGHT YELLOW	13 MEDIUM PINK	20 PALE GREEN
2 YELLOW	7 LIGHT PEACH	14 DARK PINK	21 LIGHT GREEN
3 PALE VIOLET	8 PEACH	15 LIGHT TURQUOISE	22 MEDIUM GREEN
4 LIGHT VIOLET	9 LIGHT ROSE	16 DARK TURQUOISE	23 YELLOW GREEN
5 MEDIUM VIOLET	10 ROSE	17 LIGHT SLATE BLUE	24 LIGHT OLIVE
6 DARK VIOLET	11 PALE PINK	18 MEDIUM SLATE BLUE	25 MEDIUM OLIVE
	12 LIGHT PINK	19 DARK SLATE BLUE	26 DARK OLIVE

ARRANGE FURNITURE LIKE A PRO

How many times have you hesitated to change the look of a room because of the physical work involved? Professional decorators can't take the time to actually move furniture around a room, and neither should you.

The professionals push paper patterns around a floor plan to find the best arrangement for the furniture. It's a sure way to get a working solution with the least effort. Use our templates and graph paper (or purchase more of your own), gather together a pencil, ruler, wood or metal tape measure and scissors and you're ready to begin.

The first step is the most important because careful, exact measurements are a must. Use a metal tape measure along all walls, following around all architectural features like fireplaces, radiators and built-in pieces. Measure doors and windows from their outside edges, and keep track of where the electrical outlets are.

On ¼" graph paper, draw the outline of the room, using a scale of ¼" square equals 1 square foot. Indicate windows, doors, electrical outlet positions and all other architectural features on your plan. It is also helpful to indicate the direction doors open and the position of overhead lights and wall shelving units.

The next step is to measure your furniture—the approximate sizes of pieces you plan to purchase as well as those you already have. Match the measurements of the furniture as closely as possible to the templates on page 114, or draw your own, using a scale of ¼" equals 1 foot. On tracing paper, copy the shapes of your furnishings from the templates, color them in with a dark color and cut them out. Now you are ready to begin arranging your furniture with your floor plan and patterns.

To come up with the best solution, there are several basic guidelines to follow:

● PLAN TRAFFIC PATHS to allow for easy movement within a room. Stand in the doorway of a room and analyze the natural paths to another door, a window, a closet and chest of drawers or a seating area, and don't put a piece of furniture in the way of that path. Major traffic paths (in a hall, to the front door, to a closet) should be four to six feet wide; minor ones should be planned as direct, convenient and logical routes and should be two to four feet wide.

● ALLOW CLEARANCE ROOM to pull out drawers and chairs, to make a bed, to open doors and cupboards and to get in and out of seats. Use the chart on this page to check the amount of clearance space to leave for typical situations in room arrangements.

● TAKE ADVANTAGE of architectural features in a room to serve as focal points. A fireplace, large bookcase or large window is a natural setting for a conversational grouping. Or, use your furniture arrangement to disguise a feature you don't like. For example, a horizontal emphasis will break up the length of a long room.

● CONSIDER THE NEEDS and uses of the room and group the furniture according to the function it is to serve. Each grouping within a room should be able to function as a separate unit, with traffic able to go all the way around.

● BALANCE AND LINE are two important elements to keep in mind. Consider the weight of a large piece of furniture, such as a sofa or bed or dining room table, and let it serve as the dominant piece in the room. Balance it with another large piece or smaller pieces in the room such as chairs, small tables or larger lighting fixtures. Visual weight is important here; an overstuffed chair appears much heavier than an open one, just as velvet appears much heavier than satin or a woven tweed fabric. Use the lines formed within each piece of furniture to flow to the next piece and to join the groupings within a room.

● KEEP A SPACIOUS FEELING in the room with the way you place your furniture. With a larger room, place some pieces in the center. Large pieces of furniture should be kept parallel to the walls, but smaller pieces can add variety if they are placed at an angle. Leave enough space around each piece so that a person will feel comfortable to get up and leave.

Following these simple guidelines, try several arrangements until you get the feeling that the room plan is balanced, functional and natural. Leave your final plan for a day or so and then study it again. When you are satisfied that you have the best arrangement possible, it's time to start moving the actual pieces of furniture to follow your floor plan. Make sure to keep all of your patterns and your room layout drawing when you are finished; then you'll have a head start for the next time you're ready for a change.

AVERAGE FURNITURE SIZES AND CLEARANCE SPACES

LIVING ROOM

Sofa	36" x 89"
Love seat	30" x 60"
Easy chair	33" x 32"
Cocktail table, round	40" diam.
Cocktail table, rectangle	60" x 16"
End table, square	25" x 25"
End table, round	30" diam.
Flat-top desk	52" x 24"
Secretary	36" x 19"
Bookcase	35" x 12"
Upright piano	20" x 50"
Grand piano	54" x 60"

Clearances

major traffic path	4' to 6'
minor traffic path	2' to 4'
foot room between seat and edge of table top	1'
floor space in front of chair or sofa	1½' to 2½'
chair or bench space in front of desk or piano	3'

DINING ROOM

Table, rectangle or oval	60" x 40"
Table, round	48" diam.
Straight chair	18" x 18"
Arm chair	21" x 21"
Buffet	56" x 18"

Clearances

space to get into chairs	2' to 3'
traffic path around table for serving	1½' to 2'

BEDROOM

Twin bed, head and footboard	39" x 75"
Full bed, head and footboard	54" x 75"
Queen bed, head and footboard	60" x 80"
Night stand	22" x 18"
Chest of drawers	36" x 18"
Easy chair	33" x 32"

Clearances

space for making bed on 3 sides	2'
space between twin beds if parallel or in an L-shape	2'
space to pull out drawers	3'
space for dressing	3' to 4' sq.

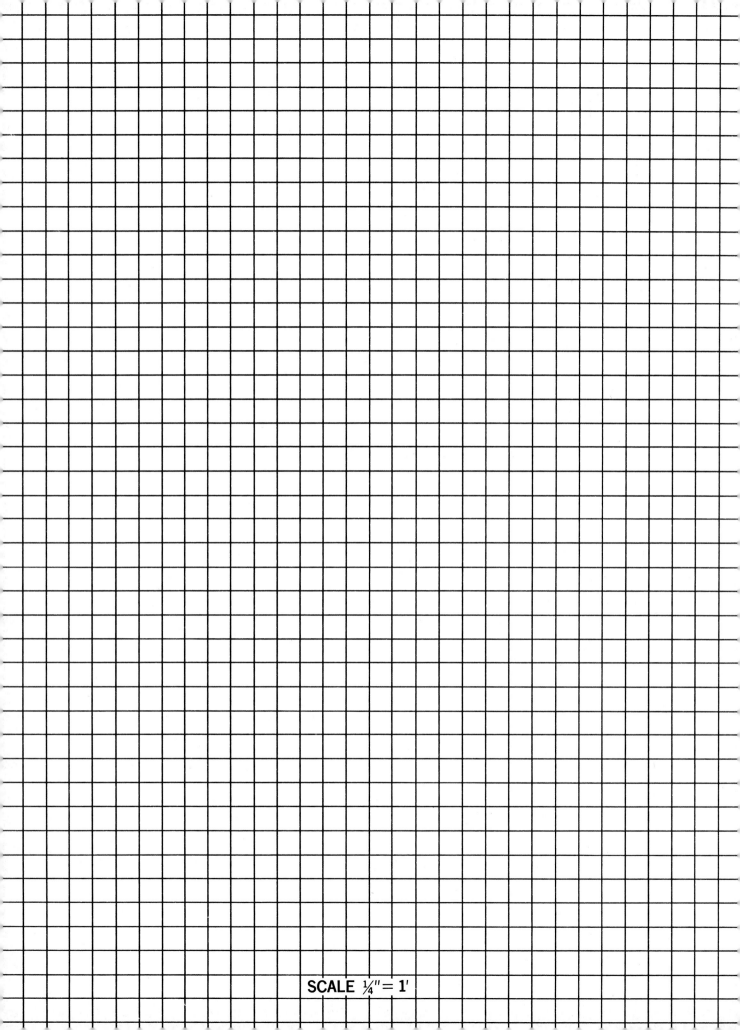

SCALE ¼"= 1'

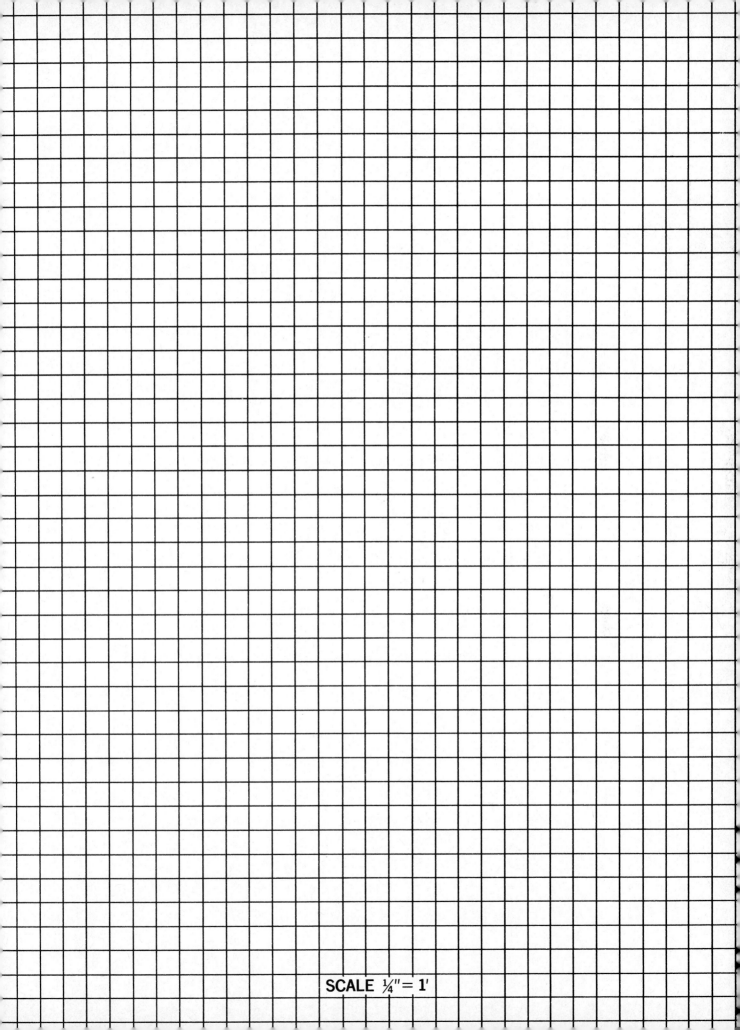

SCALE ¼"= 1'

ARRANGE FURNITURE LIKE A PRO

Use these handy template patterns with the graph paper on the previous pages to arrange the furniture in your living room, dining room or bedroom the easy and professional way. ¼" = 1'

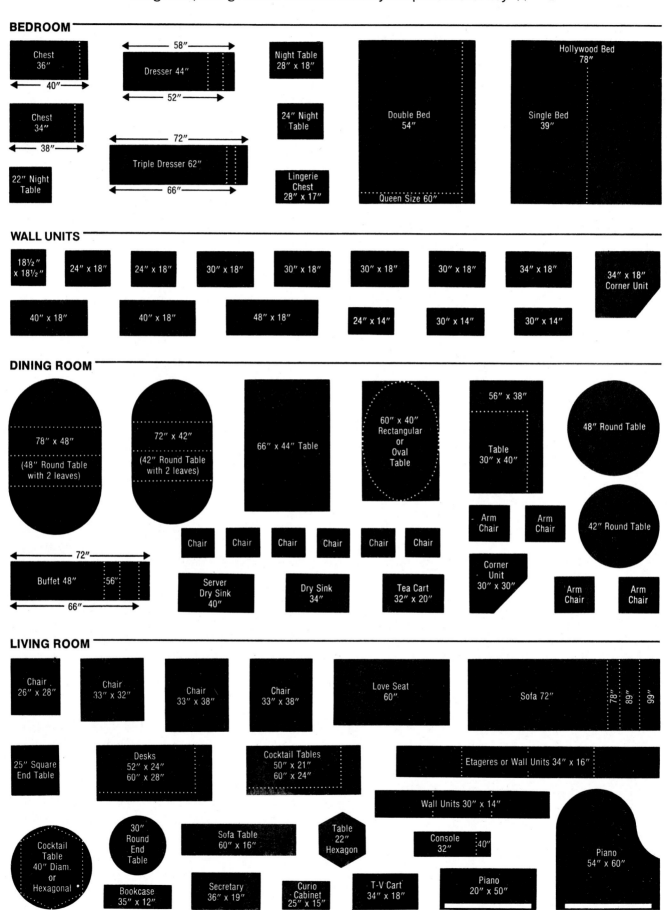

BEDROOM

Chest 36" / 40"
Dresser 44" / 58" / 52"
Night Table 28" x 18"
24" Night Table
Chest 34" / 38"
Triple Dresser 62" / 72" / 66"
22" Night Table
Lingerie Chest 28" x 17"
Double Bed 54" / Queen Size 60"
Hollywood Bed 78" / Single Bed 39"

WALL UNITS

18½" x 18½"
24" x 18"
24" x 18"
30" x 18"
30" x 18"
30" x 18"
30" x 18"
34" x 18"
34" x 18" Corner Unit
40" x 18"
40" x 18"
48" x 18"
24" x 14"
30" x 14"
30" x 14"

DINING ROOM

78" x 48" (48" Round Table with 2 leaves)
72" x 42" (42" Round Table with 2 leaves)
66" x 44" Table
60" x 40" Rectangular or Oval Table
56" x 38" Table 30" x 40"
48" Round Table
42" Round Table
Chair / Chair / Chair / Chair / Chair / Chair
Arm Chair / Arm Chair
Corner Unit 30" x 30"
Arm Chair / Arm Chair
72" Buffet 48" / 56" / 66"
Server Dry Sink 40"
Dry Sink 34"
Tea Cart 32" x 20"

LIVING ROOM

Chair 26" x 28"
Chair 33" x 32"
Chair 33" x 38"
Chair 33" x 38"
Love Seat 60"
Sofa 72" / 78" / 89" / 99"
25" Square End Table
Desks 52" x 24" 60" x 28"
Cocktail Tables 50" x 21" 60" x 24"
Etageres or Wall Units 34" x 16"
Wall Units 30" x 14"
Cocktail Table 40" Diam. or Hexagonal
30" Round End Table
Sofa Table 60" x 16"
Table 22" Hexagon
Console 32" / 40"
Piano 54" x 60"
Bookcase 35" x 12"
Secretary 36" x 19"
Curio Cabinet 25" x 15"
T-V Cart 34" x 18"
Piano 20" x 50"

OFFICE-IN-A-CLOSET

(page 117)

(**Note:** This unit is designed to fit a standard 2′6″ x 6′8″ opening.)

MATERIALS: One ¼″x4′x8′ hardboard; 32′ of 1″x12″ pine; one ¾″x27½″x29″ birch plywood; 72″ of 1″x4″ pine; plastic sliding door track for ¼″ doors (27⅝″ required); one 24″ continuous hinge; one 2″ butt hinge; 4 adjustable shelf supports; 1 flush ring pull; 1 folding table support; 1 hook and eye; 1 roll of 1″ birch veneer tape; white glue; contact cement; Minwax® wood stain; 1½″ finishing nails; white latex paint; paint brush; wood chisel; razor blade or utility knife; fine sandpaper; drill.

DIRECTIONS: Cut all the parts to size as indicated in the diagram. Assemble the top and bottom to the sides to form a frame, using white glue and finishing nails. Add the remaining fixed shelves, spaced as indicated by the dimensions, using white glue and finishing nails. Drill ¼″ diameter holes, ½″ deep, for the adjustable shelf. The hole spacing shown gives a good adjustability range. At this point, stain the unit before adding the back, desk and doors. Center the 24″ continuous hinge on the shelf facia, ¾″ down from the top edge, securing it with the screws furnished. Cut the plastic sliding door track to size and install. Trace the ring pull outline on the desk top and with a wood chisel and hammer carefully relieve the area in order to fit the ring pull flush with the surface. Using contact cement, mount the 1″ birch veneer tape to the edges. Trim with a razor blade or utility knife and sand with fine sandpaper to feather the edge. Stain the leg components to match the cabinet. Position the fixed portion of the leg to the underside of the desk, using white glue and finishing nails. Now join the remainder of the leg assembly, utilizing the 2″ butt hinge. Next mount the folding table support to assure the leg will stay perpendicular to the desk. Attach the desk to the unit. Mount a small hook and eye to the underside of the desk (put the eye on the desk) and the leg to hold the leg in the folded position while the desk is not in use. Prepaint the back and sliding doors (add finger holes to facilitate opening) before installing.

MAKING DRAPERIES WITH FABRIC

You can add a decorator's touch to rooms by choosing fabric to go with your rug, sofa, chairs and wallcovering, then making draperies that fit each window perfectly.

MATERIALS: Drapery fabric; fabric for lining; yardstick or metal tape measure; matching thread; pleater tape; dressmaker pins; pleater hooks; sharp scissors.

DIRECTIONS—Determining the Amount of Fabric Needed:

1. Draperies are measured to fit window hardware, rather than the window itself, so install hardware if it is not already in place.
2. Decide the length you wish the draperies to be. (The usual lengths are to the window sill, window apron or floor length, subtracting ½″ to clear the floor and more, if there is baseboard heat.)
3. With yardstick or metal tape measure, measure the length from the top of the drapery rod to the chosen length for the draperies; to this add 7″ for hems and length taken up by fullness.
4. Measure the width of drapery rod; add the distance from bend in rod to wall, the space for the overlap (if it is a traverse rod) and 3″ for side hem. This number doubled is the fabric width required for each window. If the window is 36″ wide, the distance from bend in rod to wall is 4″ and the overlap is 4″, the total width of fabric for the window would be twice the total of 36″ + 4″ (bend in rod) +4″ (overlap) +3″ (side hem), or 94″. Divide this number in half for the width of each drapery. (Since half of 94″ is 47″ and our fabric is 48″ wide, 1 width of fabric was needed for each drapery.) For wider windows, divide the drapery width by the width of the fabric and adjust to the nearest whole number for the number of panels required to make each drapery.
5. To estimate the total amount of fabric required, multiply the number of panels by the total length for each panel and divide by 36″. (If you choose floor-length draperies with 86″ + 7″ for hems, you will need twice 93″ or 186″ divided by 36″, or a total of 5¼ yds.)
6. For lining, use above fabric measurements, except reduce the width by 6″ and the length by 2½″.

(**Note:** These measurements do not take into account patterns that need to be matched. If this is necessary, measure the number of inches between pattern repeats and add this number to the length of *each* panel.)

Sewing:

1. Cut drapery and lining fabric to measured length for each panel. Sew panels together, if necessary, to obtain desired width for each drape, using a ½″ seam; press seams open.
2. Stitch a 1″ hem along lining bottom; pin drapery and lining fabrics, right sides together, along left side;

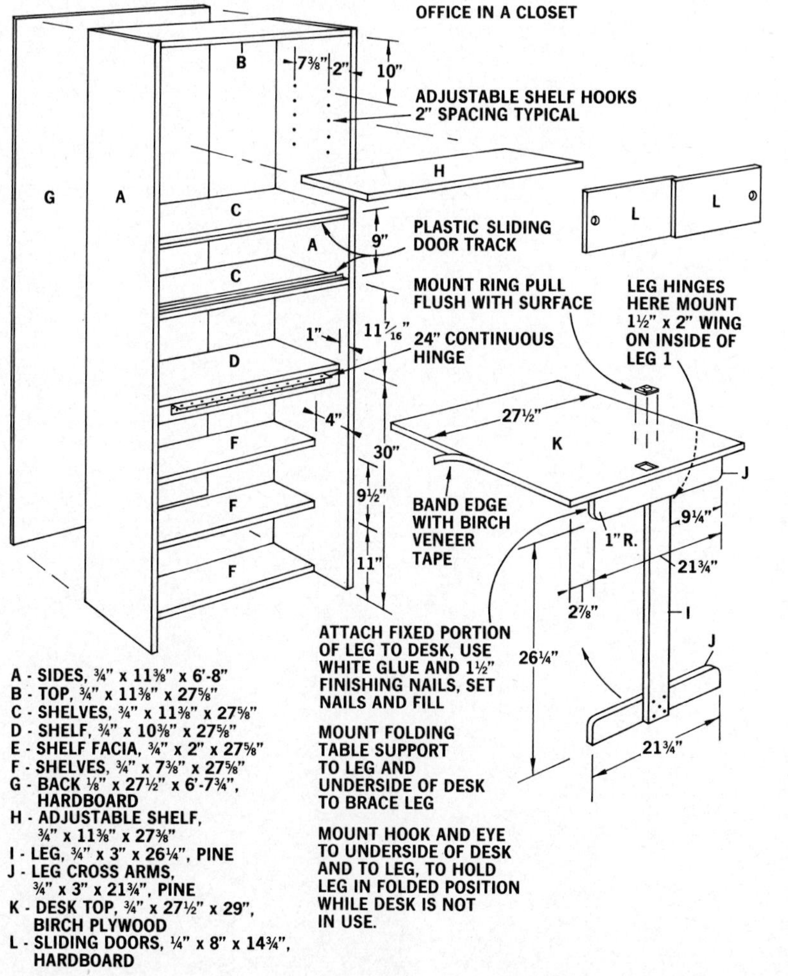

OFFICE IN A CLOSET
B
7⅜″
2″
10″
ADJUSTABLE SHELF HOOKS 2″ SPACING TYPICAL
H
G
A
C
L
L
PLASTIC SLIDING DOOR TRACK
A
9″
C
MOUNT RING PULL FLUSH WITH SURFACE
LEG HINGES HERE MOUNT 1½″ x 2″ WING ON INSIDE OF LEG 1
1″
11⁷⁄₁₆″
24″ CONTINUOUS HINGE
D
4″
27½″
F
K
30″
J
9½″
F
BAND EDGE WITH BIRCH VENEER TAPE
9¼″
1″R.
11″
21¾″
F
2⅞″
I
ATTACH FIXED PORTION OF LEG TO DESK, USE WHITE GLUE AND 1½″ FINISHING NAILS, SET NAILS AND FILL
26¼″
J
MOUNT FOLDING TABLE SUPPORT TO LEG AND UNDERSIDE OF DESK TO BRACE LEG
21¾″
MOUNT HOOK AND EYE TO UNDERSIDE OF DESK AND TO LEG, TO HOLD LEG IN FOLDED POSITION WHILE DESK IS NOT IN USE.
A - SIDES, ¾″ x 11⅜″ x 6′-8″
B - TOP, ¾″ x 11⅜″ x 27⅝″
C - SHELVES, ¾″ x 11⅜″ x 27⅝″
D - SHELF, ¾″ x 10⅜″ x 27⅝″
E - SHELF FACIA, ¾″ x 2″ x 27⅝″
F - SHELVES, ¾″ x 7⅜″ x 27⅝″
G - BACK ⅛″ x 27½″ x 6′-7¾″, HARDBOARD
H - ADJUSTABLE SHELF, ¾″ x 11⅜″ x 27⅜″
I - LEG, ¾″ x 3″ x 26¼″, PINE
J - LEG CROSS ARMS, ¾″ x 3″ x 21¾″, PINE
K - DESK TOP, ¾″ x 27½″ x 29″, BIRCH PLYWOOD
L - SLIDING DOORS, ¼″ x 8″ x 14¾″, HARDBOARD

stitch from top to within 2″ of lining bottom with a ½″ seam.

3. Pull lining fabric over so that its edge meets edge of drapery fabric; pin; stitch with ½″ seam to within 2″ of bottom of lining.

4. Center lining on drapery and press seams towards lining. Turn drapery hem up 3″ over lining; stitch ½″ seam down to bottom on each edge; turn drapery right-side out; slip stitch drapery hem. Tack facing to hem and hem to lining.

5. Turn top edge of drapery down 3″; press; pin pleater tape ¼″ down from top edge. Stitch along top and bottom of tape, keeping the cut ends turned under. *Do not* stitch pockets closed.

6. Insert pleater hooks and hang draperies in curtain hardware, arranging folds carefully.

MACRAMÉ WALL HANGING

(page 117)

Finished size is approximately 24″x40″.

MATERIALS: Wrights polyester cable cord #145-007, 1 spool white #70; Wrights spaghetti trim #1819984, 1 reel bright yellow #046; yellow spray paint to match trim; ½″ dowel, 36″ long; ⅜″ dowel, 36″ long; 4 dozen pheasant wing feathers (or other feathers approximately 6″ long); scissors; 24″x40″ brown wrapping paper for pattern; two 5″ C-clamps; quick bond glue; rubber bands.

DIRECTIONS: This wall hanging is made entirely of square knots and double half hitches. Procedure is especially important when working with long spans of unknotted cord as in this piece. The best way to ensure even tension on cords is to mount your work firmly—we suggest screwing C-clamps to a work table, about 26″ apart, then sliding the ½″ top dowel through the C's. For easy calculation of spacing between knots and of curving lines, make a full-size pattern of the diagram given. Following directions on page 37, enlarge pattern onto brown paper and place pattern under your work.

Preparing dowels: Cut ½″ dowel to 32″; cut ⅜″ dowel to make one 9″ piece and three 6½″ pieces. Spray dowels with yellow paint, using 3 or 4 coats to get a deep color.

Measuring cords: Each length is folded in half and mounted at the middle with a larkshead knot; you will have 18 yellow and 64 white knotting ends. Mount C-clamps 10 feet apart, screw side up. Tie a slipknot in end of yellow cord and tighten it around one C-clamp screw. Wrap cord around C-clamps 9 times (to make 18 cords between clamps). Tie off end temporarily. Mark center of cords (at

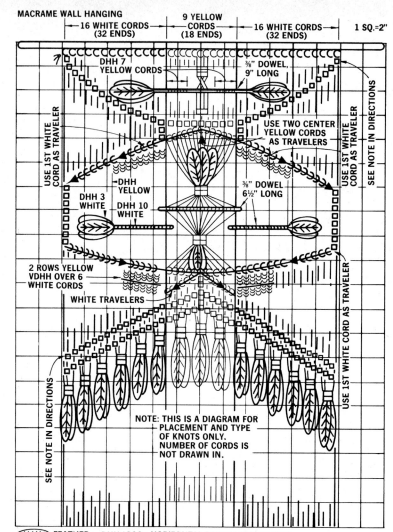

MACRAME WALL HANGING

← FEATHER   DHH/CCC = HORIZONTAL DOUBLE HALF HITCH
VHDD/ = VERTICAL HALF HITCH   □ = SQUARE KNOT   — = WHITE CABLE CORD
— = YELLOW SPAGHETTI CORD

NOTE: THIS IS A DIAGRAM FOR PLACEMENT AND TYPE OF KNOTS ONLY. NUMBER OF CORDS IS NOT DRAWN IN.

C-clamp opposite from starting point) with a piece of string. Cut cords only at end where wrapping began and ended. Spread cords apart, wind each one into a butterfly bobbin, and mount cords at center of ½″ dowel. Following same procedure, measure 32 lengths (64 ends) of white cable cord. As you cut cable cord, tie a knot or dab glue onto end of each cord to prevent raveling. Mount 16 cords (32 ends) on each side of yellow cords.

Mounting piece for working: Place C-clamps 26″-28″ apart on a work table. Place diagram on table. Run ½″ dowel through C's and pull towards you to get firm tension.

Working the knots: For top row of double half hitches, use a separate piece of cable cord for the traveler, tying a knot in one end to start row. When finished, glue ends of traveler to back of piece. Follow diagram for placement and types of knots. Do not try to count cords on diagram, since it has been simplified for easier reading. When attaching dowels, hold dowel over cords in position on diagram and work double half hitches over it. For feathers, strip downy fuzz

from quill of feather, hold in position against dowel or filler cords and knot over quill end of feather. Add a drop of quick bond glue to hold feathers securely in place.

Finishing: Trim ends of all cords following diagram (make fringe longer if desired). Untwist white cable cord to fluff out fringe. To mount, place nails on wall 26″ apart and rest mounting dowel on nails.

*(Note on square knots:** Interlocking square knots noted on the diagram are done as follows:

Starting with outer 3 cords, tie a square knot over 1 filler cord. Take next 2 cords plus inner cord of first square knot and tie second knot. If cords were numbered from outer edge, first knot would be tied with cords 1, 2 and 3; second knot with 3, 4 and 5; third knot with 5, 6 and 7; etc. Continue across work to center. Repeat from outer edge on other side.

KITCHEN FLOORING

MATERIALS: Small pry bar; hammer; tape measure; wide width vinyl flooring, at least 3 inches longer and wider than floor surface to be covered; pencil; carpenter's square or metal yardstick; shears or heavy scissors; sharp straight-bladed utility knife; metal trim, cut to length of any doorway(s) in the room.

DIRECTIONS—Preparing Floor Surface: Remove all furniture, appliances and other loose items from the room. Also remove all floor moldings, such as quarter round or cove base, with pry bar; reserve for later reinstallation. Make sure floor surface to be covered is dry, clean and free of wax build-up. Hammer flush any protruding nails and renail any loose spots. If your floor has any cracks, fill with a hard-setting, non-shrinking latex patching compound suitable for floor use. The surface should be as even as possible for best results.

Measuring and Installing Flooring:

1. Measure floor surface to be covered; make a diagram of it, including all cut-out areas.

2. Lay out flooring material in a larger room, such as your garage or basement. Using diagram as your guide, transfer room measurements to flooring material with pencil and yardstick, adding 3 inches to each side. (This ensures neater fit.)

3. Transfer flooring material to surface to be covered, lapping the 3 inch excess up walls.

4. Using utility knife, make a cut in outside corners from the top of the lapped up material to where floor and wall meet

5. With utility knife, gradually cut down flooring material on inside corners, until it fits into the corners.(see

6. Using utility knife, gradually trim down flooring material lapped up the wall until it lays flat. Do not fit flooring closer than ⅛ inch to walls or baseboard. Door trim may be slightly closer.

7. Replace molding, if any, raising it slightly from the flooring material; nail it into the baseboard, not the floor. Insert metal trims at doorways, but not through the flooring material.

OFFICE-IN-A-CLOSET

is a unique fold-away desk that provides ample room for all your home office needs and yet takes up very little space. Designed by Gary Gerber for AT&T.

MACRAMÉ HANGING

is worked entirely in square knots and double half hitches, using Wright's materials. Its natural colors would beautifully enhance a casual setting.

For project how-to's, see index on page 89.

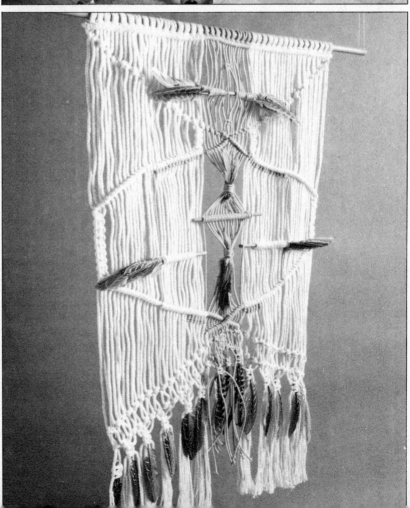

ALL
ABOUT
ANTIQUES

WHAT IS AN ANTIQUE?

New antiques are born every year. According to U.S. Customs Law, an object reaches the status of an antique when it is 100 years old. Thus, any item made in 1877 or before is now considered a bona fide antique and may enter the country from abroad duty-free. (All pieces, of course, are subject to verification by Customs. Possible exceptions include certain works of art, which may not actually have to be 100 years old to be considered antiques.) Before this change in the tariff law, the year 1830 had been (since 1930) the fixed date and inflexible yardstick in defining antiquity. Symbolically the 1830 date marked the end of an era, a convenient watershed separating the earlier hand-crafted work of independent artisans from the later mass-produced objects made in factories during the Industrial Revolution. Beyond this there is no legal definition of "antiques." An even broader view of the matter is taken in the new three-volume work on *American Antiques* published by American Heritage. It treats objects made up to the outbreak of World War I in 1914 as antiques. This viewpoint is shared more and more in the antiques marketplaces of the world.

WHERE TO BUY

It has been estimated that there are about 15,000 antiques shops of varying pretensions across America. This statistic is believable; how many miles can you drive in any direction from your home before coming onto a sign advertising antiques for sale?

Urban and small-town shops vary greatly. Some are long-established firms handling only the highest quality cabinetwork; then there's a whole range of junk, thrift, secondhand, salvage and theatrical-props shops handling the discards and crippled furniture of yesteryear. High rents force most of these dealers to be small, to specialize and to cater to the interior-decorating trade. As a result, prices tend to be somewhat high, and the stock in furniture, except for chairs and small tables, low. Large chests of drawers, four-poster beds and sofas take up too much floor space to be worth the time and effort to handle them. Because the dealer is buying his stock from a more cosmopolitan market, real artistic treasures and *objets d'art* may turn up in the course of your searching in these stores.

Country roadside shops, however, hold more promise as a happy hunting ground for the eager collector. Prices tend to be lower and the stock-in-trade much more extensive, because the country dealer can afford to be in the storage business as well as the antiques trade. In addition to being something of a local character, he is often a diligent acquisitor — attending country auctions, buying at estate sales, scouring private homes for potential purchases and even buying from other dealers. Generally he is a proud, fiercely independent businessman; he buys, sells, transports, refinishes and repairs everything in his shop. Working with his own, often limited, capital, he must of necessity have a rapid turnover of his stock so that he has money again to buy replacements for what he sells. He, therefore, often works on a fixed percentage of markup on his purchase price. If he has bought well, you can buy well, which means that these shops often have remarkable bargains if you are informed enough to distinguish the wheat from the chaff.

Another advantage of a country shop is that, wherever you find it, the stock represents the regional manufactures and tastes of the particular geographic area, largely because the dealer in question is confined to foraging and searching for antiques within a fairly tight radius of his location. It is possible to take advantage of regional specialties in building a collection. Those regions, for example, with a rich heritage in pottery or weaving or basketwork or decorative wrought ironwork will have those handcrafted traditions reflected in their antiques shops.

Auctions vary a great deal in quality and prices, according to the quality of the goods of the estate being sold. Some take place over several days, while others may only take part of a day; some may be made up of goods from one or more distinguished collections, while others may simply be the household effects and tools of a farmer. The single, most obvious disadvantage of an auction for most of us is that it is time-consuming. You must be there considerably before the start of the auction, in order to select the items of interest and to inspect their condition closely, which simply cannot be determined at a distance after the bidding begins. If there are a large number of items to be auctioned, then you must sit through the bidding on every other numbered item, waiting for the sequence of your turn.

It is easy, as experience will teach you, to be carried away by the excitement and tempo of the bidding with what is called "auction fever." (In order to avoid this and to protect their anonymity, wealthy collectors who spend tens and hundreds of thousands of dollars at auctions often prefer to do their bidding through a dealer, who acts as their agent, paid on commission.) It is a good idea to protect yourself against the emotional excitement of an auction by setting in your own mind the maximum limits that you are willing to pay on the items that interest you.

Auction prices reflect what any one person at a particular moment in time is willing to pay for a single object; they are, therefore, one of the most accurate barometers of rising or falling) prices in the antiques field. There is no truth in the assertion that antiques dealers bidding at auctions drive up market prices to their own advantage; they are simply competing with collectors in a free marketplace where there is a rising demand for a shrinking supply of antiques. The dealer must buy at what is the equivalent of a wholesale price in order to make a profit. If he outbids his competitors and pays the top price at auction for a particular piece, he must feel, at least in his own mind, that the retail or true value is greater than the auction price. The knowledgeable and discerning collector can generally make very good purchases at auctions.

The flea market is the country cousin to the urban antiques show; it lasts generally for a single day, instead of the three to five days of an antiques show, in the open air or under some sort of shed or in a warehouse. These exhibitions or bazaars are the joint effort of a number of small dealers, who show selected items from their inventory, and have the atmosphere of small-town festive, summer occasions. Because of the costs and problems of transporting their goods to such a viewing, dealers tend to bring only the smaller items and to show goods more oriented to the hobbyists. Antiques shows, on the other hand, are generally held in large cities. They give the dealer (who is there by invitation of an exhibition committee) a good chance to be exposed to a wide circle of wealthy, sophisticated collectors. Moving large pieces of furniture and setting up a booth at these shows requires a tremendous effort—and this of necessity must be reflected in the prices.

HOW TO SHOP

"The buyer needs a hundred eyes, the seller not one," the critic George Herbert has said. Learn to use your eyes! The trained eye—critical, sensitive, keenly observant—is the greatest asset of any collector. The wise collector begins from the premise of doubt—doubt concerning the genuineness and condition of a piece—until his eye tells him to think otherwise.

Learn to enter the front door of a shop with eyes scanning every corner, studying and compiling a mental inventory of everything there—rejecting the dross and remembering the small percentage of gold (or fool's gold). After reaching the back of the shop, reverse yourself and recapitulate your findings. If nothing has struck your interest by the time you have reached the front door, excuse yourself and make your exit. If there is something that interests you which is not marked, inquire at this point about prices. A few selected comparative prices will give you some idea of the general price levels of the shop. No matter how large the establishment, this type of general inventorying should never take more than a half hour— less than 10 minutes in small shops.

Practice visits to a full spectrum of antiques shops will help you develop a sixth sense about their contents from the outside looking in. Very often you can get a clue to a shop's stock by taking a good look at what's on the front porch or in the display window. A profusion of signs announcing "Chair seats caned," "Fresh cider for sale" and "We buy junk and sell antiques," for example, amid old wagon wheels, cast-iron garden furniture, a broken-down bureau covered with blistered paint, a one-horse sleigh filled with geraniums, stenciled milk cans, a rusting weather vane, give some indication of a shop's contents.

Some shops specializing in glass and china will have all their windows cluttered with cruet bottles, bitters bottles, shaving mugs, meat platters, a matching cup and saucer surviving from someone's turn-of-the-century set of wedding china and a phalanx of mismatched dinner plates. Only if the shop is big or if there is evidence of an attached barn or shed will there be much of a chance that the dealer handles a range of furniture, such as dining tables, horsehair sofas, mammoth chests of drawers, cheval glasses, wing chairs, rolltop desks and china closets—all of which take up an extraordinary amount of storage space.

Even though outward appearances do tell you something about the contents inside a shop, you should not allow the unkempt housekeeping habits of a proprietor to put you off. As one wise man has said: "There are some enterprises in which a careful disorderliness is the true method."

THE LESS EXPENSIVE ANTIQUES

Today's sharp demand for certain types of antiques keeps their prices up; high-style, first-quality rarities such as a Rhode Island block-front chest of drawers or a Duncan Phyfe sofa) and usable items for the contemporary home (brass candlesticks, pewter plates, sets of Federal period dining room chairs and Hepplewhite dining tables) have by those very virtues gone out of sight in price. American and English silver has, probably, more than any category of antiques, risen in price because of its rarity and usefulness.

But take heart—there are bargains to be found at a fraction of the cost of those stylish favorites. Special-interest, nostalgic collector's items include musical instruments, costumes, craftsmen's tools, cooking utensils, toys and dolls, clocks and watches, household hardware, sporting and gaming implements, instru-

ments of war, industrial machinery, wallpaper and architectural details, late prints and landscape paintings, shop signs and posters, and every sort of artifact surviving from the industrial, transportation and communication revolutions of 100 years ago. Since almost anything dating from the 18th century will sell at an inflated price in today's market, simply because of its rarity, more and more discriminating collectors are selecting from the profusion of 19th-century pieces and the eclectic styles that reigned in that period. In furniture alone you begin with Hepplewhite and Sheraton, then pass through the various revivals (Greek, Gothic, Egyptian, Rococo, Renaissance, Elizabethan and Turkish) and end in the confusion of Arts and Crafts, Art Nouveau and Grand Rapids. There is a world to choose from in Victorian silver, fabrics, brass, porcelain, glass, lighting devices and Oriental carpets.

Country-made furniture of the last century, made of local woods and often painted red, black, green, blue and yellow)—part of this country's folk or native art—is a highly desirable collectible today that has never been priced wildly high. The simple lines and unadorned surfaces of these rural pieces are particularly appealing to our contemporary tastes. The misguided notion that painted furniture should be stripped down to the bare wood and varnished, shellacked or oiled in the attempt to recapture the "original finish" has been the worst solecism of antiquarians and has wrecked more good pieces of painted country furniture than one would like to contemplate. A thorough, quick washing with mild soap and warm water with the aid of a vegetable scrub brush, followed by a rinse and drying, and then the application of a coat of some sort of bee's wax compound will give a painted surface the best possible treatment. The removal of old cracked varnish and shellac from old furniture is a commendable idea, so long as it can be done with brushes, cloths and paper towels and not steel wool and sandpaper. But, if possible, the original surface of old furniture should be preserved and protected.

THE TEN COMMANDMENTS OF BUYING

1. *Be suspicious of bargains when shopping for antiques.* This is the first, and sometimes costliest, lesson any collector must learn. There are bargains among antiques, yes, but anyone who sets out with a deliber-

ate determination to outwit the dealers and other collectors is sure to suffer the fall of the proud.

2. *Do not buy antiques solely as an investment.* While they have unquestionably proven to be a good investment for nearly every collector as a hedge against inflation, their rising value has depended on changing whims of taste over the passage of time.

3. *Be wary of the heavily restored and excessively refinished piece.* While every antique needs care and some restoration from time to time, a complete face-lifting can obliterate all of the signs of age which are used in judging the genuine antiquity of a piece.

4. *Be wary of reproductions and fakes.* There has been such a persistent demand for so many useful objects—such as Queen Anne side chairs, brass candlesticks and andirons, pewter porringers and spoons, silver bowls and teapots, copper teakettles, decorative wrought-iron hinges, blown-glass decanters and printed linen bed hangings, to name but a few—that prices have risen to such a level as to encourage the manufacture of "Centennial reproductions" and outright fakes.

5. *Do not haggle about prices.* While the price on a large, expensive purchase may be "elastic," most dealers consider their prices—whether marked or quoted—rigid and firm. The old business in antiques was one of trading and dealing, in which bargaining and wrangling was part of the flair and color. Today's dealer considers himself more of a middleman, a retailer of goods marked up by a fixed percentage.

6. *Study the field and learn all that you possibly can about antiques.* Subscribe to magazines and read books, attend lectures and seminars, and do not miss an opportunity to visit museums, private collections and good antiques shops.

7. *Confine your collecting instincts within manageable bounds.* You simply cannot collect within every field. And, moreover, uncontrolled and random collecting will take on a kind of blind momentum that can only result in a kind of self-defeating pack-ratism.

8. *Resist the temptation to buy mammoth objects at great distances from home.* It is only natural for elephantine antiques to sell below their proper value, largely because of the labor and expense of moving them. Unless you have access to a truck or station wagon, moving an Empire chest-on-chest, a beautifully textured millstone or a section of

wrought-iron fence can be more of a problem than you anticipated.

9. *Learn to trust the first impression of your sight and touch.* With experience, patience and persistence, you will be surprised how fully you can develop a sixth sense in judging antiques. At first glance a piece will be either convincing or questionable. The best advice I can give any-one is: If in doubt, leave it alone. This kind of instinct or hunch is a gift that must not be ignored.

10. *Collect for pleasure alone.* Let your enjoyment of collecting and owning be your only motive. The question, "Why do people collect antiques?" defies rational explanation. Men have collected antiquities, or at least classical antiquities, since before the Renaissance and the Reformation. Greater minds than ours have probed the behavioral instincts of the collector without convincing success. If you have the urge to set out upon the collector's path, don't resist it. Few avocations offer more rewards than the collecting of antiques—even if it must be on a shoestring.

—Wendell Garrett

DICTIONARY OF ANTIQUE FURNITURE

Acanthus. A conventionalized leaf ornament from the foliage of the Mediterranean acanthus herb, much favored in mahogany furniture of the neoclassical period.

Adam. A light, graceful style characterized by severe classical motifs drawn from Greek and Roman sources, introduced by Robert Adam (1728–1792) and his brother, James (1730–1794). These Scottish-born architects and designers were innovators in neoclassic patterns that were widely interpreted in the Sheraton and Hepplewhite furniture styles.

Anthemion. A stylized form of the honeysuckle flower, derived from ancient Greek art and popularized in Greek Revival architecture and Regency and Empire furniture.

Armoire. A large cupboard or wardrobe enclosed by doors from top to base and used for the storage of garments and linens (from the French, a storage piece for arms and armor).

Art Nouveau. An international style of design that flourished between 1890 and 1910. Its principal motifs were entwined vines, plant forms and female faces with swirling strands of hair. *Art Nouveau* found its chief expression in America in the work of Louis Comfort Tiffany.

Art Nouveau Lamp

Arts and Crafts Movement. A scattered, utopian, late 19th-century movement that advocated the return to the methods of hand craftsman-ship in the construction of furniture —a reaction to industrial art and design. William Morris was the major spokesman and practitioner of the movement.

Back Stool. A term used in the 17th century for a low-back, armless, upholstered side chair.

Balloon-back Chair. A Victorian chair of the Rococo Revival period with a hooped or swelling curved back with a pronounced nipped-in waistline. Balloon-back chairs were often made in sets with matching settees and sometimes in a variety of materials, even papier mâché.

Ballroom Chair. A small, delicate Victorian side chair usually made with members turned in imitation bamboo and painted in gilt.

Baluster. A turned member of columnar form, made in a series to support the railing of a balustrade or in sets for chest and table legs.

Bamboo Furniture. Furniture of the 1880's and 1890's, when Oriental designs were in vogue, with turnings made in a stylized imitation bamboo pattern. Simulated bamboo tables and chairs of American manufacture were made of bird's-eye maple and varnished; the legs of American Windsor chairs were fashioned with bamboo turnings in soft woods and painted.

Banjo Clock. A popular banjo-shaped wall clock invented and patented by Simon Willard about 1800, with a circular dial, elongated waist and rectangular base—so popular a clock design that it has been reproduced ever since.

Baroque. European design of the 17th century which tended toward exaggeration and unrestrained brilliance and virtuosity. Large alternating curves and overloaded ornament were the essence of the baroque. Twisted columns, distorted and broken pediments, and oversized moldings achieved a theatrical effect in architecture and furniture. Chairs were elaborately scrolled, tables had bases of rich sculpture, and beds were colossal structures with twisted columns and draped textiles.

Bellflower. A floral ornament of long, pointed petals popular as an inlay pattern in Federal furniture.

Belter Furniture. Laminated rosewood and mahogany furniture with lavishly carved designs and intricately pierced forms, developed by John Henry Belter, a German-born New York cabinet-maker, from 1840 to 1860. Belter furniture is in the curvilinear Rococo Revival style of Louis XV.

Bergère. A popular type of upholstered armchair in the Louis XV style. This commodious chair, with closed padded arms and loose seat cushion, enjoyed a considerable revival in the Victorian times and was known as a *Berger* chair.

Bergere

Biedermeier. A 19th-century German style of furniture (1825–1860), principally derived from French Empire forms and displaying a preference for curving lines. The term *Biedermeier* was adopted from the name of a political caricature in a

German newspaper, who typified a well-to-do, middle-class man without culture. The cabinet-work was a combination of some (not always the best features of Sheraton, Regency, Directoire, in addition to French Empire but without the excessive use of bronze hardware. Decorative supports in the form of swans, dolphins and griffins, and carved details of realistic flowers and fruits became richer and more exaggerated in the later, more sentimental period of Biedermeier.

Blockfront Furniture. New England desks and chests of drawers of the Chippendale period with alternating raised and sunken vertical surface planes. This baroque treatment was a uniquely American form of decoration and reached its perfection in the Townsend-Goddard school of Newport cabinet-making where it was known as "swelled front."

Bombé. The furniture term for swelling, rounded or bulging sides in Chippendale baroque forms; sometimes called "kettle base."

Bonheur-du-Jour. A small fitted writing table on tall slender legs, developed in France for ladies in the mid-18th century.

Boston Rocker. A rocking chair introduced around 1835 with a high back of vertical spindles beneath a wide stencil-ornamented crest rail, and with a seat curving up in back and down in front.

Boulle Work. A form of marquetry decoration in ivory, tortoise-shell, horn, brass, silver or pewter invented by the Parisian cabinet-maker André-Charles Boulle. It was introduced around 1680 and produced in large quantities in French workshops under the patronage of Louis XIV. In the 19th century, called Buhl.

Bracket Clock. A small portable or mantel clock with a short pendulum. Examples made with their own matching, decorative bracket shelf are rare.

Bracket Foot. A simple foot cut like a bracket with mitered corners, introduced around 1690 and used on case furniture.

Brewster Chair. A heavily turned armchair with rows of spindles on the back, below the arms and below the rush seat, named for Elder William Brewster of Plymouth Col-

ony. Carver chairs of the same period were simpler, with spindles only on the back.

Brewster Chair

Broken Pediment. A triangular or curved pediment "broken" by omitting the apex; a device favored by 18th-century cabinetmakers on case furniture.

Bull's-eye Mirror. A circular mirror with a convex or "bull's-eye" glass surrounded by an elaborate gilt frame, often decorated with gilt balls and surmounted by an eagle. Popular in America in the Empire period.

Bureau. A French term for a desk or secretary (**scrutoire** or **escritoire**). After 1800 in America, the term came popularly to mean a chest of drawers.

Butterfly Table. A drop-leaf table with solid hinged brackets, shaped like a butterfly's wing, to support the leaves.

Cannonball Bed. A bed of the 1820–1850 period with four heavy-turned posts, each surmounted with a ball finial, particularly favored by country turners and cabinetmakers. It had a shaped headboard and a turned blanket rail at the foot.

Canterbury. A low music rack with several vertical divisions of open-work partitions—so named because the first such piece was ordered by the Archbishop of Canterbury. Canterburies are prized today for holding periodicals and newspapers.

Captain's Chair. A low-back Windsor chair with turned, splayed legs; frequently painted.

Captain's Chest. A chest of drawers with recessed brass drawer pulls; also known as a campaign chest.

Card Table. A table made with a folding top and with a playing surface covered with green velvet or baize; appeared at the end of the 17th century and developed in the

18th. Elaborate examples frequently had depressions or sinkings at the corners to hold candlesticks and counters used in card games.

Carolean. The Restoration period in England (1660–1688) when oak gave way to walnut, the innate structural simplicity of plain Jacobean was replaced by the decorative excesses of the Baroque style, and caning took the place of solid wood panels for chair seats and backs. Pierced carving gave an added lightness in furniture. It was also the period of marquetry work and walnut veneer on pine, and of the introduction of the curved line.

Caryatid. A structured standing female figure used as a supporting column to support an entablature; a popular Empire motif.

Cast-iron Furniture. Popular 19th-century garden furniture made of hard, brittle iron cast in a mold (and distinct from wrought iron). Cast iron was also used for plant stands, umbrella racks, beds.

Cellaret. A cabinet or case with partitions, usually on legs, for wine bottles and drinking glasses.

Chaise Longue. A long couch or daybed with upholstered back, fashionable in 18th-century France. The chaise longue was known as a daybed in America from the mid-1600's, where it was an elongated bench, usually caned and covered with loose cushions.

Cheval Glass. A full-length toilet mirror (literally a "horse mirror" because it was tall enough to reflect a horse) in a freestanding four-legged frame. First made at the end of the 18th century when it became possible to cast single plates of glass six or more feet long, most cheval glasses swivel between the uprights on screws.

Chiffonière. A tall, narrow chest of drawers designed to contain personal papers, jewels, odds and ends of needlework and "chiffons" (fabric swatches).

Chinoiserie. An adaptation of Chinese motifs and a vogue for things Chinese, introduced into Europe in the 17th century through trade with the Far East.

Chippendale. A style introduced by the English cabinetmaker and designer Thomas Chippendale (1718–1779) through his book of designs,

The Gentleman and Cabinet-maker's Director, published in 1754. His furniture borrowed practically every type of design of the mid-18th century: French rococo scrolls and foliage, Chinese fretwork, Gothic traceries and classical revival pediments —all elaborately carved.

Claw-and-Ball Foot. The termination of a cabriole leg in furniture carved to resemble a bird's claw grasping a ball. Typical of the Chippendale period, this foot design was adapted from the Chinese dragon's claw holding a pearl.

Cobbler's Bench. A low, four-leg workbench used by American shoe cobblers in the 19th century; popular today when refinished as a coffee table.

Confidante. A sofa with detached easy chairs at each end. The 19th century confidante was a three-way chair, or three seats arranged in a circular fashion.

Console Table. A wall table supported by two brackets and surmounted by a mirror or pier glass.

Cottage Furniture. A general term for mass-produced Victorian furniture of simple forms, often decorated with painted stencil designs and ornamented with spool turnings.

Court Cupboard. A 17th-century term for a sideboard with an enclosed cabinet above and often an open shelf below for the display of plates and pottery vessels.

Court Cupboard

Cresting. The carved decoration at the top of a piece of furniture, such as the top rail of a chair or the head of a looking glass.

Curule Chair. A chair with X-shaped legs, derived from ancient Roman and Grecian forms used by dignitaries. These chairs were popular in Sheraton's designs and widely interpreted in the Empire period.

Dante Chair. A curule chair of the Italian Renaissance having a leather or fabric seat. The four heavy legs curve up to the arms.

Davenport. In late 19th-century America, a long upholstered sofa, often convertible into a bed. In early 19th-century England, a small writing desk intended for ladies, consisting of a chest of drawers with a sloping top.

Directoire. A transitional period (1793–1804) of furniture fashion in France between Louis XIV styles and the Empire forms of the Napoleonic era. Directoire patterns were based on Greco-Roman forms and were reflected in the designs of Sheraton in England and Phyfe in America.

Divan. An upholstered backless sofa of Turkish and Persian origin, where a *divan*—a "council of state"— came to mean a couch of many cushions on a raised platform where dignitaries of state were seated. Divans were popular in the late-Victorian period.

Dough Trough. A Pennsylvania-German trough in which bread dough was put to rise; usually on legs and made with a flat top used as a kneading surface.

Dovetailing. A cabinetmaker's favored device of joining two broad, thin pieces of wood at right angles by interlocking wedges or cleats which resemble in shape the tail of a dove.

Dower Chest. A storage chest for a bride's household linens. Distinctive American types were the Hadley chest of the late 1600's and the gaily painted Pennsylvania-German marriage chest of the late 1700's.

Draw Table. The earliest of the extending table forms of the refectory type. The leaves lie beneath the main top and, when pulled out, are made to rise and come flush with the top by tapered bearers.

Dresser. Originally a board or table on which food was dressed. In America it came to mean a chest of drawers below a mirror.

Dressing Table. From the early Georgian period, any small table with a drawer fitted with compartments and a mirror. The American term was *lowboy,* for a small dressing table and was often made *en suite* with the highboy.

Drop-leaf Table. A table with one or two hinged leaves which, when raised, are supported by a hinged leg or bracket.

Dry Sink. A kitchen cupboard with a deep well, often metal-lined, where dishes were washed; called "dry" because it was not connected with a pump or to a drain. Made in large quantity between 1820 and 1880, many dry sinks are used today for decoration in living and dining rooms.

Dumbwaiter. A serving stand with a graduated tier of rotating circular trays on a central stem, introduced in England in the early 1700's. Later, the term was used for a lift on which dishes and food passed from one floor to another.

Early American. A term used loosely by today's furniture manufacturers for simply constructed pieces of maple or pine, vaguely patterned on early country-made functional furniture. Chairs in particular are often in the slatback and Windsor forms. Devoid of carving, the rustic charm of "Early American" is achieved and its popularity sustained by simple lines and the grain of the wood.

Eastlake. A furniture fashion popular from 1870 to 1890 drawn from medieval sources and promoted by Charles Locke Eastlake in his *Hints on Household Taste* (1868). Eastlake style was characterized by straight lines and rectangular shapes, applied molding and incised carving, rows of spindling and inset tiles.

Eastlake Cupboard

Edwardian. The "Quaint" or "Picturesque" international style at the end of the late Victorian age (1900–1920). Furniture was made in a potpourri of combined styles, including the Japanese craze, Arts and Crafts, and *Art Nouveau* in their worst Continental extravagances. These parallel enthusiasms gave rise to exotic rooms in the Moorish and

Chinoiserie tastes, joiner-made furniture based on medieval Gothic forms, and pieces based on designs of free-flowing floral abstractions given to whiplash curves. Edwardian furniture lacked any unity of style.

Egyptian Revival. A style in vogue from 1820 to 1850 in furniture and architecture which featured pyramidal shapes, sphinx motifs and Egyptian columns with lotus or palm-leaf patterns on the capital.

Elizabethan Revival. A mid-19th-century style of spool-turned furniture. The ball and spiral-twist turnings were reminiscent of Cromwellian (not Elizabethan) furniture of the mid-1600's.

Empire. A style of massive, rectilinear furniture of Napoleon's reign as emperor in France. Based on styles of antiquity and concurrent with the Greek Revival in architecture, the Empire style was characterized by wreaths, urns, winged figures, clawed feet, brass mountings, rich mahogany and rosewood. Popular in America from 1815 to 1840.

Escutcheon. The decorative metal plate pierced for a keyhole.

Fan Back. A type of Windsor chair back, with the spindles flared like a fan.

Fancy Chairs. Painted and stenciled inexpensive chairs made in the classical revival patterns, usually with cane or rush seats. Popular from 1790 to 1850, fancy chairs were a prototype of the Hitchcock chair.

Fauteuil. The French term for an upholstered armchair whose arms are not upholstered (unlike a bergère).

Federal. A style combining the Sheraton, Hepplewhite and early Empire periods in American furniture, made during the early years of the Federal government (1783–1815). Among the decorative techniques employed was the profuse use of inlay (bellflower pendants, urns, ropes and tassels, conch shells and oak leaves) in a variety of contrasting woods (satinwood, ebony, rosewood, holly and curly maple). The principal carved motifs were scanthus leaves, swags and festoons, lyres and eagles.

Fiddleback. A solid chair back of the Queen Anne period in the shape

of a violin; sometimes called vase-shaped.

Fire Screen. A screen, usually painted or covered with needlework and mounted on a pole, designed to protect the sitter from the heat of an open fire.

Food Safe. A kitchen cupboard popular in rural 19th-century homes for storing food; usually with three shelves. The wooden frame had tin paneling which was pierced in decorative patterns.

French Provincial. The very simple type of farmhouse furniture used by peasants and the middle class, especially at the time of Louis XV. Made in the provinces of local walnut by unsophisticated craftsmen, these well-constructed pieces have a charming simplicity of naïve ornamentation and graceful lines that are the essence of their appeal. In the early 19th century, Louis XV curved lines and rococo motifs were mingled indiscriminately with the straight lines of the Louis XVI period, often without any hint of carved decoration to soften the angular aspects of the pieces.

Fretwork. Miniature ornamental open or pierced railings, often in the Chinese and Gothic taste, used as galleries on tables and desks by 18th-century cabinetmakers.

Gate-leg Table. An early type of table with drop leaves and extra hinged legs on either side that swing out to support the raised leaves.

Gesso. Pronounced *jesso,* a composition of chalk applied to the surface of furniture, carved in low relief and gilded.

Girandole. An elaborate wall light or bracket, often with a mirror backplate and one or more candle arms. Fashionable in England and France in the 1800's.

Girandole

Gothic Revival. A style of furniture and architecture that reflected a revival of interest in pointed arches, cusps, crockets and other medieval motifs. First in England, 1725–1750, and later in Victorian America, 1840–1865, Gothic Revival was based on a literary and ecclesiastical movement.

Grand Rapids. Enormously popular, inexpensive, mass-produced furniture manufactured in Grand Rapids, Michigan, 1890–1920. The term became synonymous with "golden oak" furniture in styles that revealed the clear imprint of the machine.

Guilford Chest. A type of chest of drawers painted over the surface in stylized flowers and running foilage and frequently found (and thought to have been made) in and around Guilford, Connecticut, 1690–1720.

Hadley Chest. An early American chest with a hinged lid and one or two drawers, decorated all over with incised floral designs in low relief. Hadley chests were made in and around Hadley, Massachusetts, 1675–1740.

Harvest Table. A long, refectory-type table popular on farms in the 1900's and used for serving farm hands at harvest time.

Hepplewhite. A style of English furniture inspired by the neo-classicism of the Adam brothers and named for George Hepplewhite. In his *Cabinet Maker and Upholsterer's Guide* (pub. 1788), Hepplewhite adapted classic ornament to furniture characterized by square tapered legs and subtle decoration achieved through inlay and carving. Chair backs were designed by the innovative use of the oval, shield and heart shapes.

Highboy. A recent term for a chest of drawers resting on a stand or frame. Not to be confused with a chest-on-chest or double chest, on low feet rather than legs.

Hitchcock Chair. A type of chair mass-produced by Lambert Hitchcock in his Connecticut factory, where the turned parts were assembled, painted to imitate rosewood and decorated with stenciled designs of fruit and flowers. Popular 1820–1860 and widely copied by other chair factories then and later.

Hoop-back. A chair back in which the uprights merge into the top rail to form a hoop, as in many Windsor chairs.

Horn Furniture. Chairs and tables made of animal horns, a style that enjoyed limited popularity in America in the late 19th century.

Hunt Board. A type of high-standing sideboard popular in southern states, 1800–1860, and used for serving food and drink to standing hunters.

Hutch. Earlier a chest or coffer for storing household goods, later a food cupbard frequently on legs. In Colonial America, the hutchtable came to mean a chair-table with a hinged top and a single storage drawer beneath the seat.

Italian Provincial. Italian country furniture, 1650–1750, made of walnut and distinctive for its imposing character, massive and rectilinear in form. Architectural details—pediments, pilasters, cornices and moldings borrowed from classical architecture—were often incorporated into the designs. Carved decoration in high and low relief and inlay work in multi-colored woods were used to enrich the surface.

Jacobean. A term for oak furniture with a solid, turned, mortise and tenon construction, rectilinear in form and decorated with geometric designs of scrolls and lunettes, carved in low relief. Associated with the reign of James I (1603–1625), Jacobean was the prototype for American furniture of the Pilgrim century.

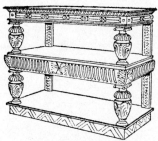

Jacobean Sideboard

Japanning. The method of imitating Oriental lacquer with paint and varnish. Japanning was used to create fanciful chinoiserie designs on raised gesso surfaces on furniture. Popular in England and America in the early 1700's.

Joiner. An early term for a furniture maker when pieces of wood were "joined" together with dowels or wooden pins (the tenons in mortise and tenon joints). Later he came to be known as a cabinetmaker when furniture was put together with metal fasteners (nails and screws) and glue.

Kas. A painted press cupboard of architectural dimensions for the storage of fabrics, generally standing on large bun feet and decorated with heavy moldings. Popular among the Dutch patroons of the Hudson Valley, 1680–1750.

Knife Box. A decorative case with its interior divided into small compartments into which knives, forks and spoons were inserted. Often made in pairs and displayed on sideboards, knife boxes had a sloping top and serpentine front into the late 1700's; they took on an urn or vase shape in the Hepplewhite and Sheraton periods.

Ladder-back Chair. A type of American Chippendale chair with horizontal curved rungs running up the back; provincial examples (often called slat-back chairs), popular into the 19th century, had as many as six graduated, ladderlike, curved slats.

Linenfold Pattern. A fashionable English panel decoration of carved folded linen, fantastically cut and shaped in oak, by French and Flemish carvers, 1475–1550.

Lion-head Mask. A decoration used by carvers on the cabriole leg knees of the early 1700's and by brasiers in brass furniture mounts in the early 1800's.

Louis VIX. The sumptuous and massive type of furniture made in the period between 1660 and 1715 (known as the *Grand Siècle*). In the 1900's revival of the style, furniture was large-scale and ornate.

Louis XV. A furniture style, 1723–1774, showing in its general design a greater suppleness—a rococo reaction against the preceding reign and its accent on asymmetry. Furniture became lighter and more comfortable. In the revival of the mid-1800's, the curvilinear, C-scroll fashions that characterized the period became popular.

Louis XV Table

Louis XVI. The period of furniture design, 1774–1793, during which the straight tapering line, oval form, and classical ornament were predominant. The refinement and delicate details of this style were revived by the Empress Eugénie in the 1850's.

Louis XVI Chair

Love Seat. A small settee for two.

Lowboy. The American term for a small dressing table. Often made *en suite* with the lower section of a matching highboy.

Lunette. A fan-shaped or halfmoon motif with carved decoration, frequently found on oak furniture of the 1600's.

Lyre. A stringed instrument motif used widely in furniture of the neo-classical and Empire periods for table supports and chair backs.

Marlborough Leg. A square leg with a block foot; the feature can be seen on some chairs and tables of the Chippendale period.

Marquetry. The process of cutting, fitting and inlaying various exotic, light-colored woods and other materials (mother-of-pearl, ivory and tortoise shell) in a darker veneer ground for application to the carcass of a piece of furniture. Floral marquetry was in vogue in England in the late 1600's; in America, a revival of marquetry took place in the lavish pieces of furniture made in the "gilded age," 1870–1900.

Méridienne. A French sofa or daybed of the Empire period with one arm lower than the other.

Mission Style. Simple rectilinear furniture, generally in "golden oak," popularized by the Arts and Crafts movement, 1890–1910, and associated with rude furnishings of the early California missions.

Monopodium. A solid three- or four-sided table pedestal, often mounted on balls or paw feet, popular from the Regency period through the 19th century.

Morris Chair. An adjustable reclining chair faced with loose cushions, invented by the English designer and craftsman William Morris in the 1860's and popular by the end of the century.

Mortise and Tenon Joint. An ancient construction technique, introduced into "joyned" furniture in the 1500's. The tenon (end of one timber) was fitted into the mortise (a corresponding cavity or socket) and secured by a wooden pin.

Mounts. Metal hardware to protect weak and vulnerable parts of furniture, such as corners and knees. French cabinetmakers of the Louis XIV period made highly decorative mounts of ormolu.

Ormolu. Ornamental, gilded forms made of cast bronze, or an alloy of brass of high purity containing zinc. Ormolu was particularly favored by the French for furniture mounts, clock cases and candlesticks. Also widely used in the 1800's on revival forms of earlier French styles.

Ottoman. An upholstered sofa with neither back nor arms, made in what cabinetmakers of the 19th century supposed to be in the Turkish manner. The term is sometimes used to describe what is little more than an overstuffed footstool. Late in the century, the ottoman became a richly upholstered circular couch with a potted palm or statuette rising from the center.

Pad Foot. The oval-shaped termination of a Queen Anne cabriole leg.

Pedestal Table. A circular table supported by a central pillar or column terminating in three club or claw-and-ball feet. Popular through the 1800's in various shapes, style and sizes.

Pediment. A triangular structure, like a low gable over a portico, used by cabinetmakers in the Chippendale period to surmount the cornices of mirrors, bookcases and chests of drawers.

Pembroke Table. A small, rectangular lady's worktable with drop-leaf sides supported by hinged brackets and usually with a single shallow drawer. Introduced in the Chippendale period and named for the Countess of Pembroke, the table was still favored in the early 1800's when Sheraton and Hepplewhite designed examples.

Piecrust Table. A round-topped table on a tripod base with a carved, scalloped, "piecrust" edge.

Pier Table. A side table meant to stand against the wall in the "pier" between windows, usually under a pier glass; often made in pairs. Introduced into America in the Empire period.

Pillar and Scroll. Widely produced machine-made furniture in the late Empire style in mahogany and mahogany veneer. Distinctive flat-sided scrolls and S-supports cut out on power-driven band saws, combined with strong simple pillars, characterize this American furniture made in the period between 1830 and 1850.

Platform Rocker. An upholstered "non-creeping" rocking chair, popular from the 1860's and often in the Eastlake style. The rockers under the body of the chair engage flat surface rails of the platform and are secured by yoke springs, bracing and leather thongs.

Prie-Dieu Chair. A low-seated chair with tall straight back with flat top on which a person's arms rest when praying.

Quatrefoil. The stylized decorative motif with four leaves set at right angles to one another within a circle; used in the Gothic Revival.

Récamier Soft. An Empire asymmetrical daybed without a complete back and having a scrolled head and foot. Named for Juliette Récamier, who, in a famous portrait by David, is shown reclining on a sofa of this type.

Refectory Table. A long table or dining board such as might have been used in the refectory of medieval monasteries; the name is now applied to long oak tables seen in the halls of domestic buildings.

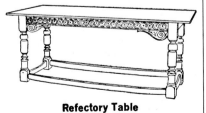
Refectory Table

Régence. In France, the period of the regency of the Duke of Orleans, 1715–1723, that saw the transition in furniture styles from baroque of Louis XIV to rococo of Louis XV.

Regency. In England, strictly the period 1811–1820, when the Prince of Wales acted as regent for his father, George III, but, in English furniture, generally allowed to be the period 1800–1835 and known as English Empire. Out of reaction against Adam's refined adaptation of the classical antique, designers advocated a doctrinaire ideal of archaeological correctness in domestic furniture of massive forms and heavy applied bronze ornament.

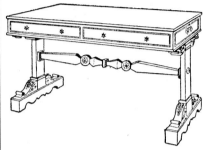
Regency Table

Renaissance Revival. A late-Victorian furniture style based on forms and motifs of the 1500's. The stiff and heavy outlines of the pieces were adorned with rounded or broken-arch pediments, sculpturesque crests and busts, applied medallions and floral motifs, all heavily carved and in high relief.

Renaissance Revival Chair

Rocking Bench. A Windsor bench or settee on rockers with a spindle gate extending across part of the front of the seat, so that a mother or nurse could rock a sleeping infant on the seat without any danger of its rolling off while she tended other light chores, such as sewing. Used widely in rural America through the 1800's. Sometimes called a mammy bench or cradle rocker.

Rocking Chair. An American invention which can be traced back to the mid-1700's; extremely popular in both England and America through the Victorian period. Most early examples were basically slat-back armchairs with rockers attached; later ones were in every sort of style and material, such as Windsor spindles, upholstery, bentwood and metal.

Rococo. A style that began in France in the 1720's and found expression in serpentine curves and asymmetrical ornament favoring shell, rock and floral forms. The extravagant use of curvilinear patterns and C-scrolls resulted in a style of inventive elegance and charming gracefulness. The term comes from *rocaille,* for the rocks and shells providing artificial decorations in French gardens.

Rococo Revival. A mid-Victorian style that modified and elaborated into novel arrangements the mid-18th-century French rococo curvilinear outlines. It exaggerated the richly carved ornaments featuring S- and C-scrolls and carved and inlay fruits and flowers.

Roll-top Desk. A massive, late-19th-century oak desk with a top of tambour construction (strips of wood glued to canvas) that rolls up into the frame.

Roundabout Chair. An armchair of the 18th century with one leg in front, one in back and the other two to each side, so that the chair could be placed in the corner of a room. Also known as a corner chair and writing chair.

Sawbuck Table. A country table with X-shaped supports.

Schoolmaster's Desk. A boxlike desk with a slant top on tall legs.

Settle. A long seat having a back and arms and an enclosed base (which often doubles as a chest, with the seat serving as a lid). Settles were especially popular in New England in the early eighteenth century.

Sheraton. A style of English furniture named after Thomas Sheraton. Through his *The Cabinet-Maker's and Upholsterer's Drawing Book* (1791–1794), Sheraton, like Hepplewhite, popularized much of the neoclassical taste in furniture in his time. In addition to his use of the prevailing classical motifs (urns, festoons, paterae and leafage), his designs were characterized by straight lines, square chair backs, squared seats and slender, reeded, tapering legs.

Sideboard. A flat-topped high table fitted with drawers and cupboards and designed to be placed at the side of a room for storage and the serving of food. Particularly popular in the Hepplewhite style after 1785 in America.

Sleigh Bed. A bed of the Empire period without posts but with a headboard and footboard of equal height curving outward, in profile like a horse-drawn sleigh.

Spanish Foot. A ribbed foot in the form of a scroll, larger at the bottom than the top, used in the early 18th century.

Spanish Plateresque. The Spanish interpretation of Italian Renaissance furniture (1500–1600). The exaggerated proportions, obvious joinery and flat turnings of this furniture made it more vigorous, more masculine than its prototype. Multi-colored painting and gilding were common and helped to cover up inferior craftsmanship. Many structures, such as refectory tables and beds, were supported with wrought-iron members. The term "plateresque" (from *platero*—silversmith) indicates the use of metal ornaments such as studded nail-heads, pierced iron mounts, and decorative hinges and hasps.

Spider Table. A gate-leg table with extremely slender legs, introduced in the Chippendale period.

Spiral Turning. Turned wooden work in the form of a twist.

Splat. The vertical member, generally shaped or pierced, between the uprights of a chair back.

Spool Turning. Turned work in the form of a succession of spools.

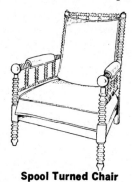

Spool Turned Chair

Stretcher. A horizontal bar uniting and strengthening the legs of a chair or table.

Tambour Front. A roll front of narrow strips of wood laid side by side on canvas backing, either for sliding horizontal doors or in rolltop covers to writing desks.

Tavern Table. A type of table with a low sturdy frame (legs and stretchers) and rectangular top generally having an overhang that's excessive in relation to the size of the frame; often with a single drawer. It is thought these tables were used in Colonial taverns.

Tea Table. A table designed to stand in the middle of the room, often with a dish top to hold the equipment for serving tea. In America, the tea table was prominent through the Queen Anne and Chippendale periods.

Trundle Bed. A small, low bed on wheels for a child or servant, which could be rolled or "trundled" under a larger bed during the day.

Victorian. The period of Queen Victoria's reign (1837–1901), when exuberant, richly carved historical styles were revived in furniture. Made by new machine processes and factory-production methods, some of the furniture may seem grotesque, if not ugly, with its florid, curved lines and sharp, angular ornaments. The copying and mixing of past styles was the one independent expression of the age.

Welsh Dresser. A side table or provincial dresser with enclosed cupboard, drawers and a ceiling-high, shelved upper structure above. Generally in oak and a traditional form in rural England from the 1600's, but the item is also associated with the Welsh settlers in Pennsylvania in America.

William and Mary. A transitional phase in English furniture fashion (1689–1702) under the influence of Dutch and French Huguenot craftsmen. It stands between the earlier straight-line, florid type of designs and the curved, plainer examples of the Queen Anne period. As a gesture to comfort, the seats and backs of chairs and settees were padded and covered in patterned velvets and elaborate needlework.

Windsor Chair. A type of chair with the back and splayed legs formed of spindles and turnings inserted in a shaped plank seat. Windsor chairs were made with an infinite variation in the design of their backs: Comb, bow, fan and arch. They were popular from the late 1700's through the 1800's.
—Wendell Garrett ■

NEEDLECRAFT STITCH GUIDE

FRENCH KNOT

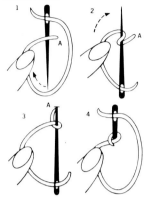

TRELLIS COUCHING

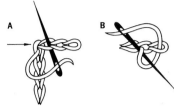

DIAMOND STITCH

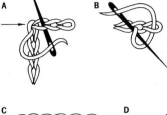

MOSAIC STITCH

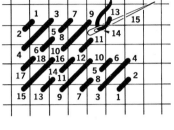

LONG AND SHORT STITCH

BASKETWEAVE STITCH

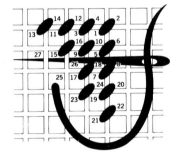

PARISIAN STITCH

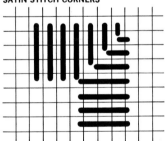

OUTLINE STITCH

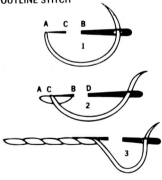

BRICK STITCH

SATIN STITCH CORNERS

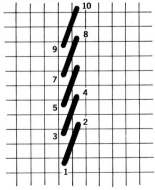

ROUMANIAN COUCHING

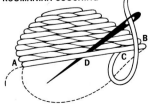

DIAGONAL MOSAIC STITCH

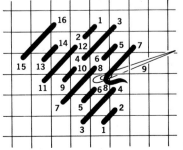

STEM STITCH